COMMON CORE MATH in ACTION

Making the Standards Manageable, Meaningful & Fun

Catherine Jones Kuhns
Marrie Lasater

Crystal Springs
SDE BOOKS

a division of Staff Development for Educators

Peterborough, New Hampshire

Published by Crystal Springs Books
A division of Staff Development for Educators (SDE)
10 Sharon Road, PO Box 500
Peterborough, NH 03458
1-800-321-0401
www.SDE.com/crystalsprings

Published 2013
Printed in the United States of America
17 16 15 14   2 3 4 5

ISBN: 978-1-935502-64-7
e-book ISBN: 978-1-935502-65-4

Library of Congress Cataloging-in-Publication Data

Kuhns, Catherine Jones, 1952-
  Common core math in action : making the standards manageable,
  meaningful & fun : grades K-2 / Catherine Jones Kuhns & Marrie Lasater.
    pages cm
  Includes index.
  ISBN 978-1-935502-64-7 — ISBN 978-1-935502-65-4 (e-book) 1.
Mathematics—Study and teaching (Primary)—United States. 2.
Mathematics—Study and teaching (Primary)—Standards--United States. 3.
Education, Primary—Curricula—Standards—United States. 4.
Mathematics—Study and teaching (Primary)—Activity programs—United
States. I. Lasater, Marrie, 1951- II. Title.

  QA135.6.K783 2013
  372.7'049—dc23

                    2013016979

Contents

Acknowledgments

Many thanks to the amazing primary teachers at Country Hills Elementary, who instill a love of learning in children every day and who allow me to be a part of the joy in their classrooms. I am honored to teach with you! —C.J.K.

I would like to thank Cindy Cliche, the rock-star teacher, who allowed me to capture the essence of a community of learners who have the freedom to risk, learn, and support each other. I appreciate McFadden School of Excellence and their primary team, who opened their classrooms to me. Thank you to the school's principal, Dr. Clark Blair, for supporting and encouraging teachers to reach their full potential. And to Clare: without you this would not be possible. —M.L.

How to Use This Book

The activities in this book are organized into five sections, one for each of the domains identified by the Common Core content standards in mathematics. Within each domain section, activities are organized by grade level, and within each grade level, by content standard.

Why are the activities grouped by domain, when the Common Core standards are grouped by grade level? Within each domain, there is significant overlap in concepts and skills across the grade levels. We decided to make it easy for you to glance through all of the activities for each domain, so you can quickly locate the best activities for your students' needs. Plus, it's helpful to revisit activities to keep skills solid from year to year.

> **Five Domains**
> Counting and Cardinality
> Operations and Algebraic Thinking
> Number and Operations in Base Ten
> Measurement and Data
> Geometry

> At the start of each domain, we set the stage for developing a deep understanding of the concepts in that domain.

DOMAIN

Operations and Algebraic Thinking

The activities in this domain build a coherent, clearly focused path for our young mathematicians to learn when it is appropriate to use addition and subtraction. They also develop strategies for adding and subtracting that instill a deep understanding of what these operations mean. We want our kindergarten students, who solve mathematical problems through acting and puppetry, to become first graders who solve problems using manipulatives and pictures, and finally to develop into second graders who are fluent in all of their math facts! The range of numbers used varies by grade level: our kindergarten students become fluent in facts to 5; our first graders master facts through 10; and their second-grade friends become fluent in all facts through 20.

When primary students have mastered simple addition and subtraction, they are not only fluent in related number facts, but they also understand the reasons for adding and subtracting and can represent these operations with the correct abstract symbols (+, −, and =). Do not rush this development; proceed clearly and slowly. Provide lots of concrete and pictorial practice with addition and subtraction, making sure that students understand the meaning of these operations before introducing number sentences written with numerals and symbols. In this way, you will give your students a solid foundation for mastering the other operations.

> Stay the course, keep on the path, give your students plenty of practice and time for discussion, and make it all meaningful and fun!

29

Domain sections contain activities for Kindergarten, Grade 1, and Grade 2. Sections are color-coded to make it easy to see which grade you're in.

Activities are organized by cluster and by content standard, within each grade level.

C-P-A stages—concrete, pictorial, and abstract—and group size suggestions are identified for each activity.

CCSSM content standards are identified for every activity. The first activity that addresses a standard has the full text of the standard; if more than one activity is provided, then later activities carry only the standard code.

DOMAIN
OPERATIONS AND
ALGEBRAIC THINKING

(K)

Whole Group,
Small Groups

K.OA.A.1 Represent addition and subtraction with objects, fingers, mental images, drawings, sounds (e.g., claps), acting out situations, verbal explanations, expressions, or equations.

GRADE(K)

Cluster K.OA.A Understand addition as putting together and adding to, and understand subtraction as taking apart and taking from.

Monkeys & Mr. Alligator

Choose six actors from the thespians in your class. One child will be Mr. Alligator and the other five will be monkeys. You may use props or puppets for the animals if you want, but it is not necessary. Talk about the five monkeys who start the poem. Say, "There are 5 monkeys and 1 alligator and they are going to act out this poem. Stand here on this stage." {Designate an area to be the "stage."} "Let's say the poem aloud and have our actors play the roles of monkeys and the alligator." As needed, describe the actions students should perform for each part.

Five little monkeys swinging on a tree
(All five monkeys swing their arms.)

Teasing Mr. Alligator, "Can't catch me!"
(Monkeys make faces at Mr. Alligator, who crawls or walks across the path of the monkeys.)

Along comes Mr. Alligator, quiet as can be
(Sneaky Mr. Alligator licks his lips.)

SNAP!
(Mr. Alligator makes a snap with arms extended toward one of the monkeys. That monkey falls down, and then he or she crawls offstage.)

Four little monkeys swinging on a tree . . .

Green Ms. Alligator demonstrates subtraction by removing monkeys hanging from a tree.

Stop here and review what the number sentence is: "There were 5 monkeys and then 1 monkey was snapped: $5 - 1 = 4$." You may write number sentences on cards in advance to show the students or write the number sentences after each snap, as the monkeys go missing one by one. For each monkey that follows, you can show two number sentences—for example, $5 - 2 = 3$ and $4 - 1 = 3$.

CCSSM CLUSTER CODES

The standards in the original print and pdf editions of <u>CCSS for Mathematics</u> contain codes for grade level, domain, and standard; for example, "1.G.2" is Grade 1, Geometry, Standard 2. Following the publication of <u>CCSS for Mathematics</u>, the CCSS writing team has added letter codes to identify the clusters at each grade level, in order to better facilitate communication and correlation. <u>Common Core Math in Action</u> uses the system that includes cluster codes. In the new system, the same example standard becomes "1.G.A.2"—Grade 1, Geometry, Cluster A, Standard 2.

We are big believers in **Math Journals** or math logs. Writing in a journal helps the writer to make sense of what he's learned and to keep track of mathematical thinking. From time to time, we suggest ways to have students record their experiences with the activities in their math journals.

Many of our activities use children's literature as a springboard for mathematics. We know the power that a well-written and beautifully illustrated story holds for a child. If we can connect what we teach and say in one academic area to another, it's a win-win situation for our kids.

It takes time to develop deep understanding—time and repetition. We've suggested **Variations** to keep activities interesting when you revisit them, or just to try if you like the variation better than the original. Of course there are those students who get it right away and beg for more. Keep them busy and deepen their understanding with **Extensions**.

Sometimes we want to share something teacher to teacher, like a **Quick Tip** about materials or a comment about related research. You'll find these notes in boxes like the one shown here.

Each grade level within each domain includes an example of an open-ended task called **See What They Know**. Used as formative assessments and as springboards for math discussion, tasks like these can serve as windows into each child's ability to tackle a problem, persevere to solve it, select appropriate tools, and answer correctly with justification for her answer. Page 5 has for tips on using See What They Know.

Math Journal: If some students are able, invite them to "record" in pictures or words what happens in this story.

Extension: Move children toward abstract representation by showing each addition sentence with its + and = signs. Write the number sentences in advance to show as you read, or write them where students can see them as you read.

Place a copy of the book at the math center and let children retell the story with party cups dressed up as ducks.

Ten Flashing Fireflies

Ten Flashing Fireflies by Philemon Sturges

This delightful story about 10 fireflies who are caught one by one is told in rhyme. Every page of this book describes a number combination, or number story, for 10. Select 10 students to be fireflies. Designate an area of the room as the jar where the fireflies are placed.

As you read this story, your 10 fireflies can flit about the classroom. But when the story tells of a firefly being captured, tap a child on the shoulder and guide him to stand "in the jar." Lead the class in a discussion about the addition sentences—for example: "There were 10 fireflies in the night sky, but 1 was caught. How many fireflies are in the night sky now? How many are in the jar? How many are there altogether? That's correct—1 firefly in the jar and 9 in the sky equals 10; $1 + 9 = 10$." Continue telling the story, stopping every time another firefly is caught. Go over each number combination, saying, for example, "There are 7 fireflies in the jar and 3 in the night sky. Who can say this number sentence for 10?"

Variation: Once you have told the story so that everyone has had a turn to be a firefly, any firefly props that you made and the book can become a center activity for literacy or math, where children can retell the story using the fireflies.

Extension: Introduce the number sentences that correlate to each part of the story. This will help children's understanding bridge to the way the number sentences look in symbols.

Whole Group, Small Groups

K.OA.A.1

Your 10 actors may wear fireflies made from craft foam, felt, or construction paper.

33

Whole Group

K.CC.C.7 Compare two numbers between 1 and 10 presented as written numerals.

✓ **QUICK TIP**
Use number lines in your class, and refer to them often. Any time you can relate the numerals to the conversation, take that opportunity!

Hop to It!

The best way to compare written numerals is to use a number line. A child can see that 4 is more than 2 because it is farther down the line away from 0. Fun objects can help children to recognize the relative positions—and relative values—of numbers from 1 to 10. For example, use plastic frogs on a number line to show the relative positions of written numbers.

- Say, "Put your frog on number 5. Put your finger on number 4. Is 4 closer to 0 than 5, or is it farther away? Right, 4 is closer to 0 than 5 is. Four is less than 5. Let's count to make sure."

- Once students understand that, say, "Now put your finger on 7. Is 7 more or less than 5 (the frog)? Right, 7 is more than 5; it is farther away from 0 than 5 is. Remember, numbers get larger as you move farther away from 0."

- Time to move the frog along the line! "Hop your frog up the line to 8. Put your finger on 5. Is 8 more or less than 5? Is 8 greater or less than 5?"

"My finger is on 4. Froggy is on 5. My finger is closer to 0 than Froggy is, so 4 is less than 5."

⊙ **SEE WHAT THEY KNOW**
Have your students solve this problem and observe their problem-solving skills. Get ready by gathering a picture of a puppy with all 4 of its legs visible and a container of small manipulatives. Choose the format that works best for your students: whole class or small groups with teacher support, or independent.

"A puppy is going out in the snow. She needs a boot to go on every paw. Can you show me the number of boots the puppy needs? Use any of the materials on the table. Count out loud so I can hear your thinking as you figure this out."

28

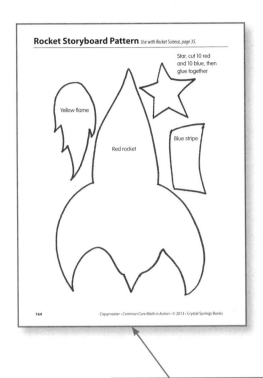

Rocket Storyboard Pattern *Use with Rocket Science, page 35.*

Star, cut 10 red and 10 blue, then glue together

Yellow flame

Red rocket

Blue stripe

164   Copymaster • Common Core Math in Action • © 2013 • Crystal Springs Books

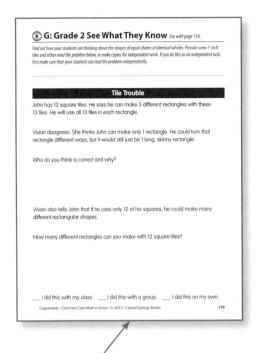

G: Grade 2 See What They Know *Use with page 154.*

Find out how your students are thinking about the shapes of equal shares of identical wholes. Provide some 1-inch tiles and either read the problem below, or make copies for independent work. If you do this as an independent task, first make sure that your students can read the problem independently.

Tile Trouble

John has 13 square tiles. He says he can make 3 different rectangles with these 13 tiles. He will use all 13 tiles in each rectangle.

Vivian disagrees. She thinks John can make only 1 rectangle. He could turn that rectangle different ways, but it would still just be 1 long, skinny rectangle.

Who do you think is correct and why?

Vivian also tells John that if he uses only 12 of his squares, he could make many different rectangular shapes.

How many different rectangles can you make with 12 square tiles?

___ I did this with my class.   ___ I did this with a group.   ___ I did this on my own.

Copymaster • Common Core Math in Action • © 2013 • Crystal Springs Books   179

We've provided some patterns to help you make some of the manipulatives mentioned in the activities. And we've provided some of the See What They Know problems as copymasters, in case you'd like to hand them out and let students follow along as you read. Patterns and copymasters are available at the back of the book.

Using See What They Know

Want to try See What They Know? It's a good idea to first read the problem aloud and, as a class, discuss what it is asking; you want the problem to provide a window on your students' mathematical thinking, unhindered by the readability of the problem.

Once you're sure everyone understands the problem, turn them loose! Tell students you want them to think and to have fun with the task. As they problem-solve, you need to circulate, listen, and offer encouragement. Remember, the first mathematical practice includes *persevere!* Take time to note what tools and strategies your students are using. Ask kids who finish early to figure out another way to solve the problem. Prompt struggling students with hints such as, "Can you show your answer on a number line?" or "Can you draw a picture or show the problem using these cubes?"

Last, call the class together for a "math meeting" and invite students to share their strategies for solving the problem. Ask each child to explain how she knows her answer is right—that explanation is almost more important than the right answer! If students in your class propose multiple ways to solve the same problem, then that is a clear signal that you have helped your students develop the thinking skills Common Core promotes.

Success with the Common Core State Standards for Mathematics

We hope you and your students enjoy these math activities as much as we enjoy doing them with our little mathematicians. All of the activities in this book support specific Common Core State Standards for Mathematics (CCSSM) at Grades K–2, and activities to support every one of the K–2 CCSSM content standard are included. These activities focus on developing the deep conceptual understanding of mathematical concepts that are the foundation for making meaningful connections, engaging in higher-level thinking, and developing rich problem-solving strategies in mathematics in the early grades and beyond.

Mathematical Practices

As you've discovered in your own experience with CCSSM, an integral part of the standards is the shift away from drill, rote, formulas, and procedure (three cheers!) to meaningful mathematics in which children make sense of problems, practice thinking skills, and develop a deep understanding of concepts.

This emphasis is evident in the importance placed on Mathematical Practices. While each grade level has specific content standards from each of the five domains, all grade levels share the same eight standards for mathematical practice. By developing these practices, we teachers can help our students develop into patient, competent problem solvers and critical thinkers. Most good math lessons utilize many of the eight practices. The correlation chart on pages 12–13 shows where in the book each of the eight standards for mathematical practice is developed.

Concrete-Pictorial-Abstract

An important aspect of Common Core State Standards is a new emphasis on student engagement in mathematics. It isn't enough to get the right answer; children need to understand and explain why an answer is correct. In order to do this, children need a deep understanding of the mathematics—not just knowing their numbers and manipulating symbols. This kind of deep understanding starts with c-p-a.

C-P-A is not a new federal agency or a type of vitamin. It is simply a way to remember the stages of reasoning: concrete, pictorial, and abstract.

- Using manipulatives is part of the *concrete* stage. Manipulatives are the best way to introduce a concept, especially in the early grades.

- After plenty of practice with concrete materials, the *pictorial* stage helps bridge the gap between concrete and abstract. Seeing pictures and drawing pictures are both good ways for children to solidify understanding of a problem or concept. The authors of Common Core are careful to point out that student drawings need not show realistic details; they just need to illustrate the mathematics.

It will come as no surprise that most activities in our book engage students at the concrete or pictorial level. After all, it's targeted for instruction of primary students, who are just starting to build mathematical concepts.

- Last to develop is *abstract* understanding—the use of numerals and symbols to represent what is happening mathematically. It's important not to rush students into the abstract stage before they are ready. If we do, the mathematical meaning may be lost, and scaffolding of more complex concepts may be destined for disaster!

C P A An icon near each activity in this book denotes whether the activity develops mainly concrete, pictorial, or abstract reasoning, or some combination of the three. Some activities and their variations may be used to develop more than one of these stages; when this is the case, plan to revisit the activity over a period of time in order for your students to reach each level.

C-P-A & COMMON CORE

Common Core is relatively new, but it is built on what we all learned in our early education classes from trailblazers like Maria Montessori, Jean Piaget, Zoltan Dienes, and Jerome Bruner: children learn best when they engage with real objects while solving real problems. The authors of Common Core also looked closely at the practices in other countries, such as Singapore, which consistently ranks at the top or near the top of all countries participating in the TIMSS (Trends in International Mathematics and Science) study. An emphasis on the concrete-to-pictorial-to-abstract progression is evident in every one of the countries with strong mathematics scores.

Making & Managing Manipulatives

We strongly recommend that you use a variety of manipulatives—and use manipulatives mats, too. Manipulatives mats help each child keep her manipulatives in one place. To create mats, start by making copies of the patterns at the back of this book. You may choose to enlarge a pattern as you copy it, if you'd like a larger mat. Cut out the individual pattern pieces and trace around the pieces on appropriate colors of construction paper. Cut out the colored pieces and glue them into place on other sheets of construction paper. If you laminate the completed mats, you can use them over and over again for years.

That is, you can use them for years if they're taken care of. We've found it's important not only to place manipulatives in a spot where children can access them easily, it is also important to demonstrate how you want classroom materials cared for and what your expectations are. Set ground rules and stick to them! Here are some suggested rules to get your students started:

- Only responsible mathematicians get to use these math tools.

- Use the math tools only in the way the teacher demonstrates.

- Never throw or chew a math tool or put it in your pocket or backpack.

- Take only what you need, and keep those tools on a work mat or at your table while you are using them.

- Always put the math tools back exactly where you found them.

When the kids are first learning how to use manipulatives and mats, we like them to sit close by, where we can easily see how they are using and treating their manipulatives.

We like to keep our manipulatives within easy reach. Clear containers let students see the contents and choose what they need. It's important to offer a variety of tools for children to choose from, so we can observe if they are implementing Mathematical Practice 5, "Use appropriate tools strategically."

Taking Time for Questions & Answers

Developing a deep understanding of mathematics doesn't happen in a day, a week, or even a month. It takes time—lots of time for introducing new concepts, thinking about them, talking about them, practicing them, and revisiting them. Children need time to discuss their mathematical discoveries, to make mistakes, and to correct each other—in short, they need time to solve problems, not just get the right answers.

Ask good questions and wait for thoughtful answers. It takes time, but it's worth it!

We can help students achieve the kind of understanding Common Core requires by asking thoughtful questions. Gone are the days when we teachers were expected to rattle off as many questions as possible for students to answer as quickly as possible. We need to ask fewer questions, and then we need to give children time to think about the questions, even struggle with them, before answering.

Marian Small suggests that teachers need to ask open-ended questions that allow any student to find something appropriate to contribute to the conversation. Our questions should leave room for a variety of strategies to be used (Small, 2012). For example, "Is the number 7 even or odd?" is not open-ended. It has one correct one-word answer and the child has a 50-50 chance of getting it right by guessing. Rephrasing the question can prompt more thoughtful responses. For example, the questions "How are the numbers 3, 7, and 9 alike?" and "How are the numbers 3 and 7 different from the numbers 2 and 8?" invite students of differing abilities to take their time to construct thoughtful responses. Questions of this type take careful planning on our part, but the results are much more revealing than *yes, no,* or another one-word answer.

Have you ever opened your mouth and said something you wish you had waited 60 seconds to say? We all have. Would your answer have been better constructed if you had waited? Probably. Well, the same is true of our students. It's important to give children time to think and reflect. Refining an answer is a skill, and that skill takes time to practice and develop.

We can almost hear you wondering, "How can I find time to slow down?" Common Core carefully scaffolds the content we are teaching our students. By addressing fewer skills at each grade level, teachers have more time to construct questions that require more thinking, and students have more time to go deeper and achieve mastery.

Making It Meaningful

Good math instruction does more than just cover content. Research has shown that for a math lesson to be successful, for students to understand and retain it, the lesson should not just involve important mathematical concepts. It should begin with a problem that is interesting, and it should connect to prior knowledge (Hiebert et al., 2000).

Engaging lessons give math meaning for students.

The goal of excellent mathematics instruction is to create and lead engaging lessons in which the students enjoy using mathematics, deepen their understanding, connect their learning to the outside world, and learn new skills. One of our favorite education quotes, simple yet profound, is from Joseph Renzulli, professor of educational psychology at the University of Connecticut and a researcher in the area of giftedness. Speaking to an auditorium filled with teachers, he said, "When the activity is engaging and entertaining, there will be more achievement." The activities in this book serve as a way for students to reach that level of joy, understanding, connection, and mastery.

Talking & Writing Mathematically

You'll notice that the activities in this book include a great deal of mathematical dialogue and writing, not only for the teacher but also for students. If they're to become solid mathematicians, children need to be able to speak and write mathematically. In order to do this, children first need to hear correct mathematical language, read mathematical writing, and take part in the writing process in a mathematical context. Here are some pointers for encouraging mathematical communication in your classroom.

- Encourage children to talk during math lessons. When children talk with one another, they are helping each other make sense of what they're learning and cementing their own understanding. Rosemary Irons, an Australian expert in helping young children understand math, has said, "Do not let them go to centers by themselves. They won't talk!"

- When you want your class to talk mathematically, tell them that. Say, "Boys and girls, I need you to discuss this with your friends using math talk." That lets your students know that you're expecting to hear only math conversations, not talk about ballet class, soccer practice, or TV shows.

- Demonstrate what "math talk" sounds like so everyone understands what's expected. Grab every opportunity to model for your students correct ways to write and speak mathematically. At first you'll need to look for opportunities: "Gee, is there a way I can add a little math talk here?" But after a little practice, we promise, talking mathematically will become second nature!

- Encourage your students to keep math journals and to fill them with drawings, sketches, and diagrams (Whitin and Whitin, 2000). If you give children simple spiral notebooks, even kindergartners can "record" in picture form what they learn. As the year goes on, your students will become better at recording what they've learned—and that is what makes a math journal such a wonderful way to show growth over time. Imagine showing a parent how a child wrote about math in September and again in April! That is pure authentic assessment.

Math journals help students see how their own mathematical understanding grows through the year.

A WORD ABOUT VOCABULARY

Some children arrive at the intermediate grades without knowing the difference between vertical and horizontal, or learning that a square is also a rectangle, a rhombus, and a polygon. That's so unnecessary! Treat your little problem solvers like mathematicians and do their future teachers a favor by using the correct terms for mathematical concepts. Call a cube a cube instead of a box. Say <u>vertical</u>, not <u>up and down</u>—or say both in the same sentence, so students understand the concept <u>and</u> acquire the mathematical vocabulary for it. Not sure what all the correct terms are? Look them up in the math glossary in the back of your textbook or in the glossary on the Common Core website, www.corestandards.org.

Expect correct vocabulary from your students, too, and praise them when they use it: "Great math language, Jaime. I like how you called it a sphere, not a ball." Or, "Wonderful, Linda. You know that the horizontal graph line is called the x-axis." Since children want to please their teachers, they will claim those terms for themselves. Kids <u>love</u> to use big words! It makes them feel smart. If they can name a dozen dinosaurs, then they can say "hexagon."

Correlation to Eight Standards

The Common Core State Standards for Mathematics include a set of eight standards for mathematical practice that should be developed at every grade level. This chart identifies where in this book each of the eight mathematical practices are developed, for each domain and grade level.

Mathematical Practice	Counting and Cardinality	Operations and Algebraic Thinking
1 Make sense of problems and persevere in solving them.	**K:** pages 18, 22, 23, 24	**K:** pages 30, 31, 32, 35, 36, 38 **1:** pages 40, 41, 42, 43, 49, 50 **2:** pages 52, 53, 54, 55, 56, 57, 58, 59, 60, 62
2 Reason abstractly and quantitatively.	**K:** page 18	**K:** pages 30, 31, 32, 38 **1:** pages 39, 42, 43, 46, 47, 48, 49, 50 **2:** pages 52, 53, 54, 55, 56, 58, 62
3 Construct viable arguments and critique the reasoning of others.		**2:** pages 52, 53, 54, 55, 56, 57, 58, 62
4 Model with mathematics.	**K:** pages 16, 17, 18, 19, 20, 21, 22, 23, 24, 25, 26, 27, 28	**K:** pages 30, 31, 32, 33, 34, 35, 36, 37, 38 **1:** pages 39, 40, 41, 44, 45, 46, 47, 48, 49, 50, 51 **2:** pages 54, 55, 56, 57, 58, 59, 60, 61, 62
5 Use appropriate tools strategically.	**K:** pages 21, 22, 28	**K:** pages 34, 37 **1:** pages 42, 44, 45, 46, 49 **2:** pages 52, 53, 54, 55, 56, 57
6 Attend to precision.	**K:** pages 16, 17, 18, 20, 21, 22, 23, 24, 25, 26, 27, 28	**K:** pages 32, 35, 36 **1:** pages 39, 49, 51 **2:** pages 52, 53, 54, 55, 56, 57, 58, 62
7 Look for and make use of structure.	**K:** pages 17, 21, 22, 23, 28	**K:** pages 37, 38 **1:** pages 39, 40, 41, 43, 44, 45, 46, 47, 48, 49, 50, 51 **2:** pages 58, 59, 60, 61, 62
8 Look for and express regularity in repeated reasoning.	**K:** pages 16, 17, 20	**K:** page 38 **1:** pages 45, 46, 50 **2:** pages 52, 53, 54, 56, 57, 59, 60, 61, 62

KEY: K–Kindergarten; **1**–Grade 1; **2**–Grade 2

for Mathematical Practice

Number and Operations in Base Ten	Measurement and Data	Geometry
K: page 68 **1:** pages 73, 74, 78 **2:** pages 86, 87, 88, 90, 91, 92, 93, 95, 96, 97	**K:** pages 101, 103, 105, 106, 107 **1:** pages 108, 110, 111 **2:** pages 118, 123, 124, 125, 126, 127, 128, 131, 133, 134	**K:** pages 136, 137, 142 **2:** pages 152, 153, 154, 156, 157, 158
K: page 67 **1:** pages 69, 71, 72, 73, 78, 79, 80, 81 **2:** pages 82, 83, 84, 87, 88, 90, 91, 92, 93, 94, 95, 96, 97, 98	**1:** pages 108, 109, 112, 113, 114 **2:** pages 121, 122, 123, 124, 125, 126, 129, 130, 134	**1:** pages 146, 147 **2:** pages 156, 157
1: pages 69, 70, 71, 81 **2:** pages 89, 95, 96	**K:** pages 104, 105, 107 **1:** pages 109, 110, 115, 116 **2:** pages 118, 121, 124, 129	**K:** pages 139, 140 **1:** page 145 **2:** pages 156, 157
K: pages 64, 65, 66, 67, 68 **1:** pages 69, 71, 72, 73, 74, 75, 76, 77, 78, 79, 80, 81 **2:** pages 82, 83, 84, 85, 86, 87, 88, 89, 91, 92, 93, 94, 95, 96, 97	**K:** pages 101, 102, 104 **1:** pages 112, 113, 115, 116, 117 **2:** pages 123, 124, 125, 126, 127, 128, 129, 130, 132, 133, 134	**K:** pages 138, 140, 141, 143, 144 **1:** pages 146, 147, 148, 149, 150, 151 **2:** pages 152, 153, 154, 155, 158
K: pages 64, 65, 66, 67 **1:** pages 74, 75, 78, 79, 80, 81 **2:** pages 82, 83, 84, 85, 90, 93, 94, 96, 97, 98	**K:** pages 100, 101 **1:** pages 110, 111, 112, 113, 115, 116 **2:** pages 118, 119, 120, 121, 122, 123, 124, 125, 126, 132, 133	**K:** pages 139, 140, 143, 144 **1:** pages 146, 147 **2:** pages 152, 153
1: pages 76, 77, 81 **2:** pages 86, 87, 88, 91, 92, 93, 95, 96, 97, 98	**K:** pages 101, 102, 103, 104, 106, 107 **1:** pages 108, 110, 112, 113, 114, 115, 116, 117 **2:** pages 118, 119, 120, 121, 122, 125, 127, 128, 129, 130, 131, 132, 133	**K:** pages 137, 138, 139, 140, 141, 142 **1:** pages 145, 149, 150, 151 **2:** pages 154, 155, 156, 157, 158
K: pages 64, 65, 66, 67 **1:** pages 69, 71, 72, 74, 75, 79, 80, 81 **2:** pages 82, 83, 94, 85, 86, 87, 89, 91, 92, 93, 94, 95, 96, 97, 98	**K:** page 103 **1:** pages 111, 115, 116, 117 **2:** pages 118, 119, 120, 133, 134	**K:** pages 136, 137, 138, 139, 140, 141, 142, 143, 144 **1:** pages 145, 146, 147, 148, 149, 150, 151 **2:** pages 152, 153
K: page 68 **1:** pages 69, 70, 71, 72, 76, 77, 79, 80, 81 **2:** pages 85, 86, 87, 93, 94, 95, 96, 97	**K:** pages 100, 101, 103 **1:** page 112 **2:** pages 118, 119, 120, 125, 126, 131	**K:** pages 143, 144 **1:** pages 149, 150 **2:** pages 153, 154, 155, 158

Counting and Cardinality

Counting is natural to children. Ask any 3-year-old which plate has more cookies, the plate with 4 cookies or the plate with 2, and the child knows right away. Anthropologists have discovered that even without formal instruction, children in remote areas of the world count in some manner.

Many children rattle off numbers when they are toddlers. Even if those numbers are not in order, that is the start of the whole counting concept. Those of us who teach young children witness these giant steps that children take before they truly understand the exactness of counting. We're sure you've observed in your own classroom the behaviors listed in the chart this girl is holding!

The last step in learning to count, knowing the total without counting, is called *subitizing*. You do this all the time. When you look at a shopping cart, for example, do you actually count each of the wheels, or do you see that cart and know the total without counting? We want our students to subitize up to 5 items by the time they exit kindergarten.

Learning to Count
- Calling out numbers in any order;
- Rote counting numbers in order;
- Touching each item and calling out a number, without missing any items;
- Understanding that the last number said is the total; and
- Looking at 4 cookies and saying, "Four!"

GRADE (K)

Cluster K.CC.A Know number names and the count sequence.

C P A
Whole Group

K.CC.A.1 Count to 100
by ones and by tens.

Count & Then Count Again & Again & Again

Count every step you take to the cafeteria, music class, the bus, the playground, or anywhere you are going as a class. Count the rungs on any ladder you see and the legs on all the chairs at one table. Just count. Say, "Let's see if we can get this room all cleaned up by the time we count to 43. Help me count." Start counting while everyone cleans. Or ask, "Will we all have our backpacks ready to go home by the time we count to 62?" How about, "I plan to read this beautiful picture book aloud.

How do you practice counting? Just COUNT!

Let's have everyone sitting criss-cross applesauce on the rug by the time I count to 84 so I can begin. Help me count: 1, 2, 3 …" Make counting more like fun, less like drudgery.

C P A
Whole Group

K.CC.A.1

Let It Roll!

Let's say your students are working on counting to 5. Make it fun. Have the kids sit in a circle. Point to one child at a time, going in order, without skipping anyone in the circle. The first child you point to says, "One." The second child says, "Two." The third child says "Three," and the fourth child says, "Four." When the fifth child says "Five," then everyone says "ROLL," as all the boys and girls roll their hands paddy-whack style, with fists clenched and hands circling each other. Continue around the circle as long as you like. This repeated practice helps children anticipate when 5 will be called so they can all say "ROLL!" When you point at each child as the number is called, you also reinforce the one-to-one number-and-object correspondence that is so important.

Another way to do this is to have the children call out numbers 1 to 6, but the sixth child says, "BOP!" and JUMPS UP! Children love this activity because they are all hoping to be the one who gets to say "BOP!" and jump. Another way to vary this is to have the class count 1 to 5, clapping on each count and adding a great big STOMP! on the number 5. Who doesn't like to make a big, loud, obnoxious noise?

Try using these activities to practice counting to any number. It may seem like a simple approach, but you are laying the groundwork for the concept of multiples. Can you count by 5s all the way to 35 by rolling, bopping, or stomping? Of course!

Fingers & Toes

Whole Group

K.CC.A.1

Kids are carrying around two perfect sets for counting by 10s. Call up six children. Say, "I was wondering how many toes are in this group?" Point to each child, counting toes by 10s as you go. Try this for counting digits on the hands as well, either by 5s or by 10s.

The Hundred Chart

Whole Group

K.CC.A.1

This amazingly simple chart packs a powerful punch. By pointing to each number as you count, you lay the groundwork for students to understand and use the helpful patterns in our number system. Find a hundred chart online. Hang hundred charts all over the classroom, glue them into the children's math journals, and hang them on the bathroom mirrors. No, we are not kidding! The kids cannot miss how important the hundred chart is if they see it when they wash their hands!

Of course the most obvious and important pattern is the repeating 10s. To point out the 10s, shade in the numbers 10, 20, 30, 40, 50, 60, 70, 80, 90, and 100, using a color that is easily visible, yet light enough for the numbers to show through. Point to the numbers as you chorally chant "10, 20, 30 . . ."

Hundred Chart

1	2	3	4	5	6	7	8	9	10
11	12	13	14	15	16	17	18	19	20
21	22	23	24	25	26	27	28	29	30
31	32	33	34	35	36	37	38	39	40
41	42	43	44	45	46	47	48	49	50
51	52	53	54	55	56	57	58	59	60
61	62	63	64	65	66	67	68	69	70
71	72	73	74	75	76	77	78	79	80
81	82	83	84	85	86	87	88	89	90
91	92	93	94	95	96	97	99	99	100

Introduce the hundred chart early, and have fun with it often!

C P A
Whole Group

K.CC.A.2 Count forward beginning from a given number within the known sequence (instead of having to begin at 1).

Catch the Count-on Jar

After children have had lots of practice counting up from 1, they are ready to try "counting on" from another number. All you need for a count-on jar is a clean, clear plastic jar with a lid (the kind used to package Parmesan cheese or peanut butter) and counters of some sort. Let's say you are working on counting on from 6. Gather students in a circle so they can see what you're doing. Then say, "Help me count the cubes as I drop them into the jar. Ready? 1, 2, 3, 4, 5, 6. That's 6 cubes in the jar, right? We counted 6." After dropping every cube, twist the lid closed and say, "There are 6 cubes in this jar. I am not going to add any more cubes or take away any cubes. The 6 cubes are going to stay there." Shake the jar to make a great rattling noise and say, "This is 6!" Tell students, "Now I want to know, what is 2 more than 6? I can start with 6 and then say the numbers that come after 6." Shake the jar and say, "6!" again, loudly, then follow with two smaller, quieter shakes and say "7, 8" with each softer shake.

Next, toss the jar to a student in the circle (it won't break; it's plastic) and say, "What is 3 more than 6?" As the child catches the jar, or picks up the dropped jar, the child calls out "6!" with a loud shake and then says "7, 8, 9" with three soft shakes. Have the student toss the jar back to you, and then toss it to another student in the circle with another question about counting on from 6. Repeat this activity on other days, using different numbers of counters in the jar.

A clear plastic jar and a few small objects help kids learn to count on from any number you choose.

 QUICK TIP

Many children, when asked, "What is 2 more than 7?" will smile and then count on their fingers from 1. When they reach 7, they then count "1, 2" more fingers. Only then do they start the whole process over again to reach 9! Counting on is tough; there is no denying it. But it's worth taking the time to help students master this skill because it is a foundational concept for both addition and subtraction.

Sandpaper Numerals

Individuals

K.CC.A.3 Write numbers from 0 to 20. Represent a number of objects with a written numeral 0–20 (with 0 representing a count of no objects).

This pure and simple tactile experience is especially helpful for children who are not yet familiar with the steps for writing each numeral. Use scissors to cut numerals from sheets of sandpaper, making each numeral at least 5 inches tall. Use a red crayon or permanent marker to draw an arrow on the numeral at the spot where students should start to write. Glue each numeral to a piece of card stock. Ask children to start at the arrow and trace each numeral with a pointer finger.

 **QUICK TIP**

Cutting sandpaper will dull your scissors, so use a pair that you don't care about.

Clay Numerals

Individuals

K.CC.A.3

Place "ropes" of clay (thin clay or Play-Doh that has been rolled to resemble a rope) and laminated number cards at a center. Consider using an inexpensive plastic place mat to help keep the table clean.

Ask children to place the clay ropes on top of the number cards to "draw" the numerals. A child who does not need the number cards for reference can simply use the clay ropes to create the numerals.

 **QUICK TIP**

Make sure students know your expectations: model how to handle each material; show children where to sit or stand; and tell them in advance which of their creations they can take across the room to show you, and which should stay at the station.

Tactile experiences help students practice "writing" numerals while they are still learning to write.

C P A
Individuals

K.CC.A.3

Fingers in Sand

Pour sand or uncooked Cream of Wheat into the bottom of a shallow plastic storage container that measures at least 8×10 inches. Be sure that the sand is deep enough to hold a mark from a finger dragging through it. Let children "write" the numerals 1 to 20, one at a time, in the sand or Cream of Wheat. The container must stay flat on the tabletop to prevent spills. To erase the numbers, either shake the box gently or smooth the sand by hand. Snap the lid back on top to store the sand for another day.

Writing in the sand— a small box of sand in the classroom or a sandy area outdoors—is a great way to practice how to form numerals.

C P A
**Whole Group,
Individuals**

K.CC.A.3

Counting Fish

 Fish Eyes: A Book You Can Count On by Lois Ehlert

This colorful book makes a great read-aloud. After reading the book to the class, give each child a sheet of grid paper, or a sheet of paper with wide lines. Each child also needs something to write with, as well as fish stickers or a fish stamp and ink pad. Have children write the numerals 0 to 9 in a column down the left side of the paper, one numeral for each line. To each line, they should add the number of fish stickers or stamps shown by the numeral—no fish for the 0 line, one fish for the 1 line, and so forth. You may prefer to have children add the fish as they write each numeral.

Math Journal: Have children draw the appropriate number of items to match each numeral. They may choose whatever animal or object is their favorite to draw.

GRADE K

Cluster K.CC.B Count to tell the number of objects.

Modeling Counting

Whenever you have a reason to count, take the opportunity to model counting for your students. Let the children see and hear you, and touch each item as you count. Place your hand on each shoulder as you count the children in line. Touch each glue stick as you count them out for an activity. Place a finger on each picture in a counting book or flip chart. Children need the reinforcement that each item is counted once—and only once—and that every item is counted.

Block Tower Game

This game combines pictorial representations of numbers with actual objects—and it's fun! For each student pair, prepare a set of nine game cards by drawing dots or placing small stickers to represent the numbers 1 to 9, using domino dot arrangements. Mix up each deck so that the numbers are not in order.

Give each pair of children access to a container of blocks (all the same size) and a deck of nine dot cards, placing the cards dot side down. Children take turns flipping over a card, counting the number of dots or stickers on the card, and then building a tower with that many blocks, again counting the number of blocks as they build. When a child takes a second turn, he adds the matching number of blocks to his tower.

Children may play to find out who builds the tallest tower, or they may play to simply build towers.

Whole Group

K.CC.B.4 Understand the relationship between numbers and quantities; connect counting to cardinality.

Pairs

K.CC.B.4a When counting objects, say the number names in the standard order, pairing each object with one and only one number name and each number name with one and only one object.

Variation: Instead of building a block tower, the child forms a path or trail by laying down the same number of tiles or blocks as the number of dots or stickers on the card.

Extension: Once students are solid on written numerals, move to practice with abstract symbols by giving them decks of cards with the numerals 1 to 9. Children build towers with the number of blocks that matches the number on the card.

C ▶ P ▶ A
*Small Groups,
Individuals*

K.CC.B.4b Understand that the last number name said tells the number of objects counted. The number of objects is the same regardless of their arrangement or the order in which they were counted.

How Many Ways?

This one works well as a center activity or in small groups. Ask children to count several sets of 5 items. Then arrange the 5 items different ways and count again. You will want to demonstrate first how 5 frogs can be 3 plastic frogs in the top row and 2 plastic frogs in the bottom row, or 2 plastic frogs in the top row and 3 plastic frogs in the bottom row, or a circle of 5 frogs, or any other arrangement. Say, "Boys and girls, I know you are so smart. How many ways can you show 5?" Leave a variety of items at a center table and let the counting begin!

Extension: An easy transition to the pictorial stage of this activity is for the child to draw the arrangements with dots and then draw a loop around each set of 5.

"How many different ways can you arrange 5 items?"

Fill the Plates

Label each of 10 paper plates or bowls with one number, 1 to 10. Place them at a center, along with a large quantity of manipulatives. At the center, the child places 1 item on the 1 plate, 2 items on the 2 plate, 3 items on the 3 plate, and so forth, until each plate is filled with the correct number of items. As the child fills each plate, she counts the objects aloud starting at 1. The next child at the center has the task of

"Fill the plates with the correct number of items for each written numeral."

checking the last child's work. He does this by counting the number of items on each plate to determine if the plates were filled correctly, then emptying the plates and filling them himself.

C **P** **A**

Individuals

K.CC.B.4c Understand that each successive number name refers to a quantity that is one larger.

Touch & Count

Remember that children are not naturally organized, so they need to see how you organize items when you want to count them before they try it for themselves. Spread out a number of small objects or counters. With the children watching, line up the objects in some organized manner, such as in one horizontal line, in one vertical line, or in an array. Then ask, "How many items do we have here? Let's count them." As you count each item, touch it. Remind the children that you want to be sure to count all of the items, and you want to be careful not to count any item more than once. Change the number and configuration of the objects and count again. When students seem to have the hang of it, provide counters to small groups so they may practice themselves.

C **P** **A**

Whole Group, Small Groups

K.CC.B.5 Count to answer "how many?" questions about as many as 20 things arranged in a line, a rectangular array, or a circle, or as many as 10 things in a scattered configuration; given a number from 1–20, count out that many objects.

K.CC.B.5

K.CC.C.6 Identify whether the number of objects in one group is greater than, less than, or equal to the number of objects in another group, e.g., by using matching and counting strategies.

> ## ✔ QUICK TIP
>
> *We like to provide a nonexample to our students every once in a while, such as double-counting an item or not counting an item. Hearing one of our charges pick up on the teacher's goof makes us smile inside. Hearing them explain the teacher's "mistakes" to their classmates is a great way to hear how they think. Their friends also get to hear the same message from a different source. If you do this, and no one catches your mistake right away, then "double-check" your work until someone catches on.*

Counting Out Frogs

Place at least 20 manipulatives for counting, let's say frogs, on a table. Say, "Who will show me 8 frogs? Count out loud so that I can hear your great counting!" Encourage the children to softly count along if your volunteer needs support. After the frogs are counted, return the frogs to the pile, change the number to be counted, and choose a new child to count out the frogs. This simple little activity can be repeated over and over again with different items to count. It is also an easy and productive way to fill in three or four minutes waiting for school pictures, the bus line, or lunchtime!

GRADE Ⓚ

Cluster K.CC.C Compare numbers.

The best way to compare one set to another set is by using one-to-one comparisons. The following one-to-one comparisons use the best manipulatives—KIDS! Start out by asking, "Who likes apples, and who prefers oranges? Kids who like apples better line up over here, and kids who like oranges better line up over there." (You may use any appropriate question to sort the children into two lines: "Who walks, and who rides in a bus?" "Who's wearing sneakers, and who has another kind of shoe today?") Let kids move to the spots you have directed. Ask, "Which group looks like it has more people?" Allow kids to come up with some answers, but don't count the groups yet.

Ask the children who like apples to stand in one line with their shoulders touching. Ask the children who like oranges to stand in another line facing the apple kids. Make sure that the first child in one line is standing directly across from the first child in the other line. Now you are ready for some fun one-to-one comparisons.

London Bridge

After sorting the kids into two lines, say, "Apple kids put your arms up like you're playing London Bridge. Orange kids put your arms up so that your hands touch the hands of the student across from you. Is anyone without a friend from the other line to form a bridge with?"

The children will let you know right away if this is the case. "See, the line with more children is also the line with people who can't form a bridge. That shows us that the line of children who like oranges has fewer people than the line of children who like apples." After pointing this out, count the students in the lines to confirm your conclusion. Say something like, "Yes, 14 is more than 8." Always go back and count the number of items in each set when making this kind of comparison.

You'll have lots of opportunities to compare numbers when you sort your children into two lines using fun questions. Sometimes the two lines will be equal, like this. Other times, one line will be longer than the other.

MORE FUN QUESTIONS FOR FORMING TWO LINES

Here are some more question suggestions for these activities:

- *Who likes cheese pizza? Who likes pepperoni pizza?*
- *Who prefers watermelon? Who prefers popcorn?*
- *Who is wearing short sleeves and who has long sleeves?*
- *Who has a collar and who has no collar?*
- *Who is getting lunch in the cafeteria and who has a lunch box?*
- *Who has a shirt with letters on it and who does not?*

Whole Group

K.CC.C.6

Feet to Feet

Use the two "fruit" lines or re-sort the children using a different question that has only two answers. With the children in two facing lines, say, "Sit down and put the svoles of your shoes against the soles of the person across from you. Who has no one to touch shoes with? That means your line is longer. There are more children in your line. The number of children in your line is greater than the number of children in the other line."

As soon as one line runs out of other kids to partner with, it's clear which line is longer—and which number is greater.

✓ QUICK TIP

Let the children hear you use math language along with more familiar language: "This line is longer, so that means the number of children in this line is greater than in that line." Or "This line is shorter, so the number of children in this line is less than in that line." Always go back and count to confirm the statement.

Shoulder to Shoulder

Sort the children into two lines, as described on page 24. With the two lines side by side, have the children turn so they are facing the back of the person who was standing next to them in the same line. Then say, "Touch your shoulder to the shoulder of the friend across from you." If some children find that they have no one to touch, that means their line is longer, and there are more kids in their group.

Variation: Elbow to Elbow; this is just like Shoulder to Shoulder except children's elbows touch.

One to One on the Table

The previous four activities demonstrate how to compare the sizes of two sets, using large-movement kinesthetic and tactile experiences. Your kids can easily transfer these experiences to comparing sets of smaller items.

Place two sets of counters on the tabletop—let's say plastic teddy bears, some red, and some blue. Ask children to guess which set of bears has more items. Once the kids have made their guesses, make a straight line of red teddy bears. Then line up the blue bears next to the red ones. Ask, "Which line is longer? Which one has more bears?" Go back and count the bears in each line—that is, the items in each set.

When the children have seen enough demonstrations, form pairs, provide objects, and have the children in each pair compare the sizes of their sets. Use buttons, bottle caps, stuffed animals, or any items you have available. Give the kids ample opportunities to compare a variety of items from different sets. Always go back and count the items in each set.

The bears not paired belong to the set with the greater number of bears.

Variation: Another way to demonstrate this concept is to pile the sets of bears, without lining them up. Remove a blue bear and a red bear from their respective piles. Take a second blue bear and second red bear and so on until all of the bears of one color have been matched with bears of the other color.

27

> **K.CC.C.7** Compare two numbers between 1 and 10 presented as written numerals.

✔ **QUICK TIP**

Use number lines in your class, and refer to them often. Any time you can relate the numerals to the conversation, take that opportunity!

Hop to It!

The best way to compare written numerals is to use a number line. A child can see that 4 is more than 2 because it is farther down the line away from 0. Fun objects can help children to recognize the relative positions—and relative values—of numbers from 1 to 10. For example, use plastic frogs on a number line to show the relative positions of written numbers.

- Say, "Put your frog on number 5. Put your finger on number 4. Is 4 closer to 0 than 5, or is it farther away? Right, 4 is closer to 0 than 5 is. Four is less than 5. Let's count to make sure."

- Once students understand that, say, "Now put your finger on 7. Is 7 more or less than 5 (the frog)? Right, 7 is more than 5; it is farther away from 0 than 5 is. Remember, numbers get larger as you move farther away from 0."

- Time to move the frog along the line! "Hop your frog up the line to 8. Put your finger on 5. Is 8 more or less than 5? Is 8 greater or less than 5?"

"My finger is on 4. Froggy is on 5. My finger is closer to 0 than Froggy is, so 4 is less than 5."

👁 SEE WHAT THEY KNOW

Have your students solve this problem and observe their problem-solving skills. Get ready by gathering a picture of a puppy with all 4 of its legs visible and a container of small manipulatives. Choose the format that works best for your students: whole class or small groups with teacher support, or independent.

"A puppy is going out in the snow. She needs a boot to go on every paw. Can you show me the number of boots the puppy needs? Use any of the materials on the table. Count out loud so I can hear your thinking as you figure this out."

Operations and Algebraic Thinking

The activities in this domain build a coherent, clearly focused path for our young mathematicians to learn when it is appropriate to use addition and subtraction. They also develop strategies for adding and subtracting that instill a deep understanding of what these operations mean. We want our kindergarten students, who solve mathematical problems through acting and puppetry, to become first graders who solve problems using manipulatives and pictures, and finally to develop into second graders who are fluent in all of their math facts! The range of numbers used varies by grade level: our kindergarten students become fluent in facts to 5; our first graders master facts through 10; and their second-grade friends become fluent in all facts through 20.

When primary students have mastered simple addition and subtraction, they are not only fluent in related number facts, but they also understand the reasons for adding and subtracting and can represent these operations with the correct abstract symbols (+, –, and =). Do not rush this development; proceed clearly and slowly. Provide lots of concrete and pictorial practice with addition and subtraction, making sure that students understand the meaning of these operations before introducing number sentences written with numerals and symbols. In this way, you will give your students a solid foundation for mastering the other operations.

Stay the course, keep on the path, give your students plenty of practice and time for discussion, and make it all meaningful and fun!

GRADE Ⓚ

Cluster K.OA.A Understand addition as putting together and adding to, and understand subtraction as taking apart and taking from.

Ⓒ ▸ Ⓟ ▸ Ⓐ

*Whole Group,
Small Groups*

K.OA.A.1 Represent addition and subtraction with objects, fingers, mental images, drawings, sounds (e.g., claps), acting out situations, verbal explanations, expressions, or equations.

Monkeys & Mr. Alligator

Choose six actors from the thespians in your class. One child will be Mr. Alligator and the other five will be monkeys. You may use props or puppets for the animals if you want, but it is not necessary. Talk about the five monkeys who start the poem. Say, "There are 5 monkeys and 1 alligator and they are going to act out this poem. Stand here on this stage." (Designate an area to be the "stage.") "Let's say the poem aloud and have our actors play the roles of monkeys and the alligator." As needed, describe the actions students should perform for each part.

Five little monkeys swinging on a tree
(All five monkeys swing their arms.)

Teasing Mr. Alligator, "Can't catch me!"
(Monkeys make faces at Mr. Alligator, who crawls or walks across the path of the monkeys.)

Along comes Mr. Alligator, quiet as can be
(Sneaky Mr. Alligator licks his lips.)

SNAP!
(Mr. Alligator makes a snap with arms extended toward one of the monkeys. That monkey falls down, and then he or she crawls offstage.)

Four little monkeys swinging on a tree . . .

Stop here and review what the number sentence is: "There were 5 monkeys and then 1 monkey was snapped: $5 - 1 = 4$." You may write number sentences on cards in advance to show the students or write the number sentences after each snap, as the monkeys go missing one by one. For each monkey that follows, you can show two number sentences—for example, $5 - 2 = 3$ and $4 - 1 = 3$.

Green Ms. Alligator demonstrates subtraction by removing monkeys hanging from a tree.

Math Journal: If some students are able, invite them to record in pictures or words what happens in this story.

Variation: Like all good read-alouds, this poem can become a center activity. Write the poem on chart paper or a laminated card and place it at the center, along with small toy monkeys and a toy alligator (or pictures of monkeys and an alligator) and let your students retell and act out the poem.

Monkeys on the Bed

*Whole Group,
Small Groups*

K.OA.A.1

Choose five actors to be monkeys, one actor to be Mama, and one actor to be the doctor. Explain to the monkeys that they are going to be "naughty monkeys" and jump on the pretend bed (an area that you designate as the "bed"). Read this poem for the children to act:

Five little monkeys jumping on the bed
(All five monkeys are jumping.)

One fell off and bumped his head.
(One monkey lies on the floor.)

Mama called the doctor and the doctor said,
(Mama pretends to talk on phone and doctor answers.)

"No more monkeys jumping on the bed!"
(Doctor shakes his first finger and head.)

You say, "There were 5 monkeys and 1 fell off the bed. What is that number sentence? That's right, $5 - 1 = 4$. There are fewer monkeys now than there were before because we are taking away monkeys." Continue this song to 4 little monkeys jumping on the bed, then 3 little monkeys, and so on.

 **QUICK TIP**

Most children are natural-born actors who delight in acting out books, poems, and stories. The puppets that we create for our class dramas become manipulatives for a child or two children to use in retelling the story at math centers or reading centers. Is it reading or math? The answer is "Yes!"

**Whole Group,
Small Groups**

K.OA.A.1

Five Speckled Frogs

Select five students to be the speckled frogs. Designate a spot on the floor as a "speckled log." You can use a rectangle made of banner paper, poster board, or ribbon, or just use an imaginary line. Designate a place for the "pool," which can be blue fabric, blue poster board, or imaginary.

Speckled frog actors take their places sitting on the log, froggy style.

Five green and speckled frogs

Sat on a speckled log

Eating some most delicious bugs.

YUM-YUM
(Kids rub their tummies.)

One jumped into the pool,
(One frog hops into pool.)

Where it was nice and cool,

Now there are four green speckled frogs.

Stop this song to ask, "What is the number sentence here? There were 5 frogs on the log and 1 jumped off. That's right, 5 − 1 = 4." Continue to sing until there are no more green speckled frogs left on the log and the number sentence is 1 − 1 = 0.

**Whole Group,
Small Groups**

K.OA.A.1

Quack and Count

 Quack and Count by Keith Baker

Read this story once for enjoyment, and then enlist seven students to play the roles of ducks as you read the story once again. Duck actors may wear simple duck beaks if they would like costumes. As you tell this story, the number of ducks stays the same. It is always 7. However, the combinations change. Each part of the story is a number bond (number combination) for 7. When there are "3 ducks and 4 ducks," ask the children, "What is the addition sentence for 7 on this page?"

Math Journal: If some students are able, invite them to "record" in pictures or words what happens in this story.

Extension: Move children toward abstract representation by showing each addition sentence with its + and = signs. Write the number sentences in advance to show as you read, or write them where students can see them as you read.

Place a copy of the book at the math center and let children retell the story with party cups dressed up as ducks.

Ten Flashing Fireflies

 Ten Flashing Fireflies by Philemon Sturges

C P A

Whole Group, Small Groups

K.OA.A.1

This delightful story about 10 fireflies who are caught one by one is told in rhyme. Every page of this book describes a number combination, or number story, for 10. Select 10 students to be fireflies. Designate an area of the room as the jar where the fireflies are placed.

As you read this story, your 10 fireflies can flit about the classroom. But when the story tells of a firefly being captured, tap a child on the shoulder and guide him to stand "in the jar." Lead the class in a discussion about the addition sentences—for example: "There were 10 fireflies in the night sky, but 1 was caught. How many fireflies are in the night sky now? How many are in the jar? How many are there altogether? That's correct—1 firefly in the jar and 9 in the sky equals 10; 1 + 9 = 10." Continue telling the story, stopping every time another firefly is caught. Go over each number combination, saying, for example, "There are 7 fireflies in the jar and 3 in the night sky. Who can say this number sentence for 10?"

Variation: Once you have told the story so that everyone has had a turn to be a firefly, any firefly props that you made and the book can become a center activity for literacy or math, where children can retell the story using the fireflies.

Your 10 actors may wear fireflies made from craft foam, felt, or construction paper.

Extension: Introduce the number sentences that correlate to each part of the story. This will help children's understanding bridge to the way the number sentences look in symbols.

*Whole Group,
Individuals*

K.OA.A.1

Ten Little Fish

 *Ten Little Fish* by Audrey Wood

This cleverly illustrated story told in a delightful rhyme starts with 10 fish and demonstrates subtraction as the fish leave one by one. When all but 1 fish has left, it becomes an addition story as the last fish meets 1 more fish.

You will need 12 actors. Ten actors will be little fish; one actor will be Mama fish; and one will be the fish who joins at the end of the story. Read the story aloud and let the children illustrate it through their actions. Discuss the number sentences that describe the changes during the story.

Variation: Set up a center activity with this book, a simple drawing of a pond, and either plastic fish or goldfish crackers. Children may retell the story themselves.

*Whole Group,
Small Groups*

K.OA.A.1

Instant Presto Number Stories

As you work on number combinations, use the canvas of your classroom as your storyboard to make up real-life number combinations. If you are working on number 4, call up 4 students and say the same number combination several different ways. For example:

- There are 4 kids here; 2 are girls, and 2 are boys. That's right— 2 and 2 is 4; 2 + 2 = 4. There are 4 kids total.

- There are 4 children; 1 child is wearing glasses, and 3 are not. That's right, 1 and 3 is 4; 1 + 3 = 4.

- There are 4 kids; 3 are wearing Velcro shoes, and 1 is wearing laces.

- There are 4 kids; 2 children are wearing blue jeans, and 2 are wearing beige pants.

- Ask the class, "Can you find any other combinations?"

Kids love this approach because it is all about them, and everyone can participate. They love to find out details about each other. Emphasize the whole (the total number of kids in the group) and the parts (the subgroups that add up to the whole).

Coloring Book

Simple pictures, such as the ones available for this activity on pages 160–163,
are the coloring-book equivalent of number bond stories. These are pictorial experiences that encourage discussion of number combinations. For example, when the child has finished coloring, ask her to describe the fish in terms of a number combination. She may say something like, "I have 6 fish; 4 fish are blue and 2 are green. That makes 6 fish; 4 + 2 = 6." Another child may say, "I have 6 fish; 1 fish has bubbles, 5 fish do not; 1 + 5 makes 6!"

*Small Groups,
Individuals*

K.OA.A.1

Rocket Science

By using themed manipulative mats, or storyboards, children can tell stories to their center partners about the action they create on their math storyboards. Make a rocket storyboard like the one shown, and foam or paper stars that are red on one side and blue on the other. A pattern for this storyboard is available on page 164.

Begin the activity by modeling stories that contain number combinations for any number up to 10. Say, "My rocket zoomed through space. I looked out my window and saw 5 red stars and 2 blue stars! There were 7 stars in all." Another example: "My rocket raced by the sun. I looked out the window and saw 1 blue star and 3 red stars. That makes 4 stars."

Pairs

K.OA.A.2 Solve addition and subtraction word problems, and add and subtract within 10, e.g., by using objects or drawings to represent the problem.

With storyboards like this one, children can tell number stories while stretching their imaginations.

C ▶ P ▶ A
Pairs, Individuals

K.OA.A.2

Butterfly Storyboard

You can make a butterfly storyboard like the one shown here using the pattern on page 165. Include some foam butterflies that are yellow on one side and pink on the other: Here are some ideas for using the storyboard: "It was a beautiful day! I saw 4 pink butterflies and 3 yellow butterflies sipping nectar from the flowers in my garden. There were 7 butterflies taking a drink from the flowers." Or, "A little hummingbird saw 5 yellow butterflies and 2 pink butterflies resting on the petals of the flower. That means there were 7 butterflies in all."

Four pink butterflies and 3 yellow butterflies make 7 butterflies on this flower.

C ▶ P ▶ A
Pairs, Individuals

K.OA.A.2

Bear & Buzzy Bee Storyboard

Make a Bear & Buzzy Bee storyboard and 7 bees, using the patterns on page 166. Use it to tell your students stories using number combinations to 7: "Poor Bear! He has 4 bees buzzing around his head and 3 bees on his nose. Poor Bear! He has 7 bees buzzing around him!" Or, "Poor old Bear! He has 7 bees buzzing near his ear and no bees in the air. Poor Bear is bothered by 7 bees."

A storyboard with craft-foam bees lets children act out all of the number families of 7. You can change the number of bees so children can practice different number families.

Spaces for Ten

The pattern for this necktie-shaped storyboard appears on page 167. There are 10 spaces on this tie, but you can make the pattern work for any number by changing the number of spaces and writing the desired number in the triangle. Next to the tie-shaped storyboard, place a small bag with 10 red dinosaurs and 10 green dinosaurs. If you do not have dinosaurs, you can use anything from cubes to counters, as long as there are 10 each of two different colors. The child reaches into the bag, pulls out an item, places it on a space on the tie, and repeats until all 10 spaces have been filled. Once the spaces are filled, the child arranges the counters so that like colors are together. Then she can create any kind of outrageous story that matches the counters such as, "I had to babysit 10 loud and wild dinosaurs for their mother. There were 10 dinosaurs: 7 were green and 3 were red. Boy was I tired!" When one partner is finished, then the other has a turn.

Small Groups, Pairs

K.OA.A.3 Decompose numbers less than or equal to 10 into pairs in more than one way, e.g., by using objects or drawings, and record each decomposition by a drawing or equation (e.g., $5 = 2 + 3$ and $5 = 4 + 1$).

 SEE WHAT THEY KNOW

Let your kindergartners show you their thinking skills with this quick task. Let them work the way that is best for your class: whole class or small groups, with or without teacher support. Give each child 10 small objects to be the ants and a grooved ruler to be the log. Tell the children what each object represents, and then have them line up their ants on their logs. Ask the children to make up stories about their ants. For example, a child may say, "There were 2 ants on the log. They invited 4 more ants to join them for a picnic. 2 ants plus 4 ants equals 6 ants at the picnic." Children may use less formal language, too, such as "2 ants and 4 ants are 6 ants."

Spaces for Races

Make a storyboard that shows a raceway finish line. You also need 20 little race cars, 10 each of two different colors. You can use two colors of small plastic cars from a novelty store, or make paper or craft-foam cars in two colors. When you introduce this storyboard, let children hear you model a math story like this one: "There were 10 cars at the finish line: 7 cars were red, and 3 cars were yellow. There were 10 cars in all." Or, "There are 10 cars in the race. There is 1 red car, and there are 9 yellow cars."

Pairs, Individuals

K.OA.A.4 For any number from 1 to 9, find the number that makes 10 when added to the given number, e.g., by using objects or drawings, and record the answer with a drawing or equation.

C P A
*Whole Group,
Pairs, Individuals*

K.OA.A.4

Ten Cups Upside Down

Nothing could be much easier than this one. Have your students sit in a circle on the floor. Place 10 plastic cups right side up where everyone can see them. Say, "There are 10 cups. Watch me." Turn 3 cups upside down and then say, "There are still 10 cups, but 3 cups are upside down. How many cups are right side up?" Allow kids to count. Many children at this age point as they count. Praise the ones whom you notice double-checking their counts. "I love how some of you counted two times to be sure you were correct. That is so smart of you!" After praising your students, take answers from your class, and confirm correct answers: "Yes, there are 10 cups and 3 cups are upside down. That leaves 7 cups right side up."

Repeat this over and over, using different number combinations for 10, reminding children that there are always 10 cups total. Once children are comfortable with this activity, the cups may be placed at a math center for extra practice.

"Zero cups are right side up and 7 cups are upside down. 0 + 7 = 7!"

C P A
*Whole Group, Small
Groups, Individuals*

K.OA.A.5 Fluently add and subtract within 5.

Number Bracelets

Give each student a pipe cleaner and the same number of plastic beads as the number the class is studying. If you're working on adding and subtracting up to 5, give 5 beads of the same color to each child. That way, color won't distract children from the numbers. Later, you can use another color for bracelets with a different number of beads.

Have each child thread the beads onto her pipe cleaner and then twist the ends together in a circle, so the beads don't spill all over the floor. Next, have the children separate the beads into sets on the bracelet to create number sentences. For example, if a child has 5 beads on a bracelet, she can separate them into a set of 3 and a set of 2 to show that 3 + 2 = 5. When you tell the children to flip their bracelets over, they'll see that 2 + 3 = 5. If they take their 5 beads and separate them into sets of 2 (with 1 left over), they'll show that 2 + 2 + 1 = 5. To show subtraction, students can group all 5 beads together and then slide beads to one side. For example, 5 − 3 begins with 5 beads; then the student pulls 3 beads away, leaving 2 beads.

This number bracelet shows 3 + 2 = 5. By moving the beads along the pipe cleaner, a child can see all the other combinations that equal 5, too.

GRADE 1

Cluster 1.OA.A Represent and solve problems involving addition and subtraction.

Flower Garden

This simple center activity is very tactile and absolutely set up for success. Use construction paper or craft foam for the background, grass, and leaves. Use a glue gun to attach green flowerless stems, making the number of stems equal to the number you would like your students to work on. Use two colors of paper or foam to make round two-sided flowers, or simply provide students with a set of two-sided round counters equal to the number of stems.

As the child places a flower at the top of each stem, he may say something like, "There are 7 flowers: 3 flowers are red and 4 flowers are yellow. There are 7 flowers in all." "Whole-part, part-whole" is critical as we build from understanding to fluency. Because there are only 7 stems and only 7 two-sided flowers, it is impossible to arrive at anything other than the correct answer! Hurrah!

Pairs, Individuals

1.OA.A.1 Use addition and subtraction within 20 to solve word problems involving situations of adding to, taking from, putting together, taking apart, and comparing, with unknowns in all positions, e.g., by using objects, drawings, and equations with a symbol for the unknown number to represent the problem.

Flower power! Use as many stems as the target number children are working with. Children use two-sided counters to show all the possible combinations that add up to the target number. This storyboard has 17 stems and shows 12 + 5.

Number Sentences in Your Name

This one is for children who can spell their first and last names. Before class, locate online and print out a sheet of 1-inch grid paper for each child. Each child also needs a pencil, crayons or colored pencils, and scissors. Display a sheet of chart paper and have some tape or a glue stick handy for use during the class discussion. In class, hand out the grids. Each child writes her first and last names on the grid in pencil, one letter to a square, in one long line. Each student colors the squares with her first name in one color and the squares with her last name in another color. Make sure that students can still read their names through the colors. When finished, each child cuts out her first and last names in one long strip. (Children with longer names may need to tape their first and last names together.)

- Say, "Each of you has a number sentence in your name. Look at Katie's. Her first name has 5 letters. Her second name has 7 letters. Her number sentence is 5 + 7 = 12. The total, or sum, of her number sentence is 12."

- Say, "We're going to create a chart of the number sentences in our names. We are going to start with the number sentence that has the least total and add number sentences to the chart until we reach the greatest total."

- Ask, "Is there anyone in the class with a number sentence total of 1? Why not? How about a total of 2?" Emphasize that no one has a total of 1 since it would be impossible to add all of the letters in two names and get a total of 1.

- Keep calling out numbers until the child with the fewest total letters in his name says, "That's me!" Then glue or tape the child's first and last names at the top of the chart paper. Next to the child's name, write the appropriate number sentence.

- Call out the next largest number, add any names with that total to the chart, and write the number sentence that corresponds to the number of letters in each child's first and last names.

- When there are several number sentences that equal the same number, take advantage of this opportunity. Say, "Look at this: We have four names that equal 9. Some of the number sentences are different. Tom's name equals 9, and his number sentence is 3 + 6 = 9. Marc's number sentence is 4 + 5 = 9. Sarah and Emile both have the number sentence of 5 + 4 = 9. Their sentences are different, but they all *equal* 9!"

After the chart is complete, keep it posted in your room for a while and refer to the number sentences.

Number Sentences in Our Names

GaryLin	4+3=7
EmILYROSe	5+4=9
AndreaLin	6+3=9
LisaPlosky	4+6=10
TeriElwood	4+6=10
SARAHoджаjvo	5+6=11
DanielLopez	6+5=11
ZacharyZbar	7+4=11
ReubenWalker	6+6=12
LoganGarfield	5+8=13
Jillian	7+6=13
AlexSimoneaux	4+9=13
RebeccaBailey	7+6=13
JaceMORtengen	4+9=13
Alyssacistella	6+8=14
BrandonNicolas	7+7=14
ChristianFoster	9+6=15
ALEXANDRAEPSTEIN	9+7=16
Christopher	11+10=21

Gary had the fewest letters. Christopher had the most letters.

From shortest to longest, your students' names are rich in number sentence practice! Point out multiple number combinations that add up to the same sum. This chart shows 5 names that add up to 13, with 3 different number sentences.

1.OA.A.2 Solve word problems that call for addition of three whole numbers whose sum is less than or equal to 20, e.g., by using objects, drawings, and equations with a symbol for the unknown number to represent the problem.

✓ **QUICK TIP**

Make a game out of your daily review of addition facts, and you'll make those facts stick.

1.OA.A.2

Trio Problems

Ask children to get into groups of three, or assign groups of three. You are going to pose to your students a variety of problems, all of which have three addends. Encourage your children to see each problem as a three-addend problem, and to write that problem on a dry-erase board or sheet of paper, using a box, a line, a question mark, or any other kind of symbol for the unknown total.

Trio problems to pose:

- Add up the ages of everyone in your group. How old is your group?

- What if I gave each of you enough candles for your next birthday cake? How many candles would your group need in all?

- How many letters are in everyone's first names in your group?

- How many letters are in everyone's last names in your group?

- How many buttons are on everyone's clothing?

- Let each child grab a handful of Unifix cubes, and then ask how many cubes each group is holding in all.

As they work, allow kids to grab manipulatives, to draw, or to use number sentences as they solve the trio problems. Celebrate the variety of methods your young charges use. In doing so, you validate their approaches.

Three-Addend Games

This activity builds on the trio problems but emphasizes the use of abstract symbols and numerals rather than concrete objects.

Arrange your kids into groups of three. Have some dice and number cards available. Give your students instructions along these lines:

- Roll three dice with your two partners. See who can add the three numbers most quickly. Repeat, keeping score with tally marks.

- Work in groups of three. Each person flips a number card at the same time. Who can call out the total of the three cards first? The first child to say the correct answer keeps all three cards. Continue the game until the teacher calls, "Time's up!" The winner is the player who finishes with the most cards.

GRADE **1**

Cluster 1.0A.B Understand and apply properties of operations and the relationship between addition and subtraction.

Number Houses

Before class, make one or more number houses for use at a center. Cut a sheet of construction paper roughly in the shape of a house. Make it at least 9 inches wide and 11 inches from the base to the peak of the roof. Use a contrasting color of paper to add three windows and a door to the house, each of which is slightly larger than a 3 × 3-inch sticky note. Mount the house on a larger sheet of construction paper and laminate the whole thing.

To use the number house, first place four sticky notes on each house—one on each window and one on the door. Choose a trio of numbers that are related by addition and subtraction facts. Write one number on each of the three window stickies. Let's say you use the numbers 6, 2, and 8 on the windows. The child studies the numbers. Then, on the door sticky, he writes the four number sentences that use all three of the numbers on the windows. In this case, he would write these sentences on the door sticky:

$$2 + 6 = 8$$
$$6 + 2 = 8$$
$$8 - 2 = 6$$
$$8 - 6 = 2$$

Variation: If your students need manipulatives to figure out the number sentences, allow them to use the tools of their choice. A little support goes a long way in giving students confidence as they transition from concrete thinking to abstract thinking.

Extension: Once students have worked with the houses and understand the basic idea, they may create all three windows, *and* the door, on their own.

1.0A.B.3 Apply properties of operations as strategies to add and subtract. *Examples: If 8 + 3 = 11 is known, then 3 + 8 = 11 is also known. (Commutative property of addition.) To add 2 + 6 + 4, the second two numbers can be added to make a ten, so 2 + 6 + 4 = 2 + 10 = 12. (Associative property of addition.)*

Construction-paper "houses" and sticky notes help students to learn number families. You can use the houses over and over again if they're laminated.

C P A

*Whole Group,
Small Groups, Pairs*

1.OA.B.4 Understand subtraction as an unknown-addend problem. *For example, subtract 10 – 8 by finding the number that makes 10 when added to 8.*

Ten-Frames to the Rescue!

Any 10-frame will do with this activity, but a giant 10-frame really gets the point across! You can make one using colored plastic tape on a plastic shower curtain from the dollar store. The ever-popular cheap plastic party cups work well with the giant 10-frame—or perhaps colorful plastic party plates, depending on the size of the 10-frame that you create.

Assemble the children on the floor, in a circle. Place the 10-frame in the middle of the circle.

- Discuss that there are 10 spaces in the frame and right now, "all the spaces are empty." Reinforce that there are 10 spaces.

- Place 8 cups on the 10-frame, 1 cup to a space, filling one row of 5 and the first 3 boxes of the next row. After the children count the cups in the spaces, ask, "How many spaces are there in all? That's right, there are 10 spaces."

- Next, ask, "How many cups did we place?" Allow some think time before guiding the conversation. "Hmm, there are 10 spaces and we placed 8 cups on the 10-frame, so how many spaces are empty?"

- Lead the conversation to help students generalize to the abstract number sentences that are illustrated by the 10-frame: "There are 10 spaces; 8 spaces have cups, and 2 spaces do not have cups. So, that means that 8 and 2 more are 10; 8 + 2 = 10. It also means that 10 take away 8 is 2; 10 – 8 = 2!"

Show students other number sentences using the giant 10-frame.

 QUICK TIP

Be sure to use this kind of interchangeable language when you lead discussions. Hearing multiple ways to say the same number sentence will help children make the leap from a language-driven problem to a symbol-driven problem.

GRADE 1

Cluster 1.OA.C Add and subtract within 20.

Spunky Monkeys Count by Twos

 Spunky Monkeys on Parade by Stuart J. Murphy

Stuart Murphy's *Spunky Monkeys on Parade* links counting by 2s to adding 2. After reading and discussing the book, we like to use a number line to show the children how skip-counting by 2s works. Draw an arc to show the jump from 0 to 2, and then write "+2" above the arc. Next, draw an arc from 2 to 4, write "+2" on that arc, and so on. Once your students understand what is happening, make another number line that shows only the numbers 0 and 20. Replace the numbers 1 to 19 with unlabeled hash marks, as shown. Your mathematicians can help you fill in the addition sentences under each +2 step, as well.

This terrific book supports counting by 2s!

Whole Group, Individuals

1.OA.C.5 Relate counting to addition and subtraction (e.g., by counting on 2 to add 2).

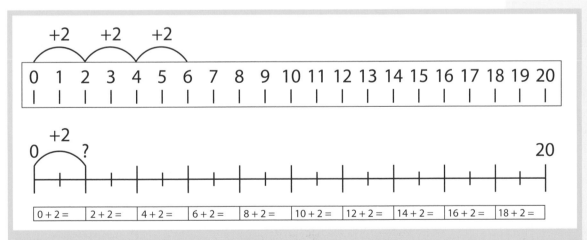

Both number lines can be displayed for a whole group using an interactive whiteboard, document camera, or chart. After your students have seen you model this, they can write on their own number lines.

Whole Group

1.OA.C.5

**Whole Group,
Individuals**

1.OA.C.6 Add and subtract within 20, demonstrating fluency for addition and subtraction within 10. Use strategies such as counting on; making ten (e.g., $8 + 6 = 8 + 2 + 4 = 10 + 4 = 14$); decomposing a number leading to a ten (e.g., $13 - 4 = 13 - 3 - 1 = 10 - 1 = 9$); using the relationship between addition and subtraction (e.g., knowing that $8 + 4 = 12$, one knows $12 - 8 = 4$); and creating equivalent but easier or known sums (e.g., adding $6 + 7$ by creating the known equivalent $6 + 6 + 1 = 12 + 1 = 13$).

Ten Little Hermit Crabs

 Ten Little Hermit Crabs by Lee Fox

As a class, read and enjoy this story that relies on subtraction and addition as part of the story line. The first read can be during your read-aloud story time. Read it again during your math time, and as you do, write where students can see the related addition or subtraction sentence for each event in the lives of the hermit crabs.

Double Ten-Frames

The 10-frame is such an easy way to help children see the way that numbers are arranged that it pays to be sure that all children are familiar with it as early as possible in their mathematical adventures. "Making a ten" is a very powerful strategy that will serve your students well when they are in the intermediate grades—if their understanding of it is solid in the primary grades. A double 10-frame drawn or glued onto both insides of a file folder is easy to make and maintain. If each child has a chance to make his own double 10-frame file folder, he will more readily use this power-packed tool. Reproducible templates for a 10-frame are easy to find with a quick online search.

It's important to model the use of the double 10-frame several times when students are first introduced to it; manipulatives also help. For example, you might use toy cars in two different colors to solve the problem $8 + 6$ with the double 10-frame:

- Say, "I am going to use the double 10-frame for this. First, I count out 8 yellow cars and 6 red cars. Watch as I drive the 8 yellow cars onto the 10-frame. Do you see how I have lined up the cars?"

- "Now, watch how I add the 6 red cars." Drive 2 of the red cars onto the same 10-frame, and park them in the empty spaces.

- Then say, "I have filled up this 10-frame, so now I must park the other 4 red cars in the other 10-frame. Do you see how $8 + 6$ is also $8 + 2 + 4$? That's called 'making a ten.' Making a ten works for other problems, too."

Demonstrate problems such as $5 + 6$, $7 + 4$, $8 + 7$, and so on.

Variation: Once your students understand what is happening, move on to using more abstract manipulatives such as chips or tiles.

Modeling 8 + 6 = 14 using a double 10-frame and small toy cars.

If You Know . . . Then You Know . . .

The concept of inverse operations is very important, so model it for your students frequently. At this level, introduce the concept informally using a simple scenario. Sit on the floor with your students with some dinosaur manipulatives and a simple blue construction paper "watering hole." Tell a story like this:

"There are 8 dinosaurs at the watering hole." (Move 8 dinosaurs to the blue paper.) "Six more dinosaurs join them." (Bring 6 more dinos to the paper.) "How many dinosaurs are together at the watering hole?"

Allow children to explain how they got their answers. (Pat yourself on the back if you hear more than one strategy from the group.) Then proceed with a related subtraction story like this:

"There were 14 dinosaurs at the watering hole. After 6 dinosaurs finished taking a drink, they moved on. Now how many dinosaurs are at the watering hole?"

Once the class has agreed on the answer, you say, "Remember we figured that 8 + 6 is 14, so 14 − 6 must be 8. What do you notice about these two number models (or number sentences)? Listen closely: 8 + 6 =14, so 14 − 6 = 8. If we know that 8 + 6 is 14, then we know that 14 − 6 is 8! How cool is that?" We want our students to be

Some children will know the answer right away, but do not be surprised if others find the answer by counting all the dinosaurs left on the blue paper. Be patient; remember that purposeful practice leads to automaticity.

looking for structure, and this is a perfect example of finding structure in number models.

Continue with more stories of dinosaurs arriving at and leaving the watering hole. Use different manipulatives so that stories and numbers change while the concept practiced remains the same.

Math Journal: Place the blue watering hole and the dinosaurs at a center for further practice. Encourage children to tell similar stories to their friends and have them connect concrete to abstract by recording the addition facts and related subtraction facts in their journals.

 QUICK TIP

Remember that the Common Core State Standards give us the go-ahead to introduce concepts informally before our students learn them formally. So don't call it "inverse operations," even though that is, in fact, what you are demonstrating when you let them discover, "If 6 + 8 is 14, then 14 − 6 has to be 8!" Early experience with inverse operations will serve your little ones well later, when they work with larger numbers, multiplication, and division.

C P A
*Whole Group,
Individuals*

1.OA.C.6

Making Tens & Doubling Up

Help students develop their number sense by showing them how to use what they know to make difficult problems easier. Use Unifix cubes in two different colors to show students how making tens can simplify a problem. Ask students, "What are some ways I can think about solving 7 + 4?" Accept all ideas. Then make a stack of 7 cubes in one color and a second stack of 4 cubes in another color. Ask students, "How many cubes do I need to turn this 7 into a 10? That's right, we need 3 more cubes; 7 + 3 = 10." Take 3 cubes from the stack of 4 and add them to the stack of 7. "We have 1 cube left over. How many do we have total? That's right, 10 + 1 = 11. So how much is 7 + 4? That's right, 7 + 4 is 11 because 7 + 3 + 1 = 11."

Use this same method to demonstrate doubles as a shortcut for solving these types of problems. Make two stacks of Unifix cubes, one with 7 cubes and another in a different color with 8 cubes. Ask, "What do you get when you add 7 and 8? Well, what do you get when you add 7 + 7?" Hold the two stacks so that there are two columns of 7 side by side. "That's right, 7 + 7 is 14." Point to the cube sticking up on the taller stack. "But 8 is 1 more than 7, so 7 + 8 is 1 more than 7 + 7. So 7 + 8 is the same as 7 + 7 + 1, or 15."

Extension: Show students how to use the same strategies to solve related subtraction problems.

 SEE WHAT THEY KNOW

Here's an example of the kind of open-ended task that you can use to assess how your first graders are doing at developing rich problem-solving skills. This problem is available as a copymaster on page 168 if you would like your students to follow along as you read. Provide paper, pencils or crayons, and 10 small objects; real acorns are nice, but any small objects will work. First, read the story aloud. Discuss what the math problem is, in the story. Once you are sure that the children understand the words and the task, let them work on it in pairs, small groups, or alone. Be sure to celebrate the different ways your students solve this problem.

"Mama Squirrel has a chore for Little Squirrel to do each day. Mama has hollowed out many holes in the tree to store nuts for the winter. Little Squirrel has to fill one hole each day. Each hole is large enough to store 10 nuts. One day, Little Squirrel finds 3 nuts by the sidewalk, 4 nuts under the big oak tree, and 2 nuts on the roof. Does he have enough to fill the hole? If not, how many more nuts does he need? Use pictures and words to show your thinking."

GRADE 1

Cluster 1.OA.D Work with addition and subtraction equations.

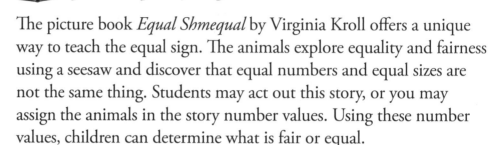

Balance Scale

Equal Shmequal by Virginia L. Kroll

1.OA.D.7 Understand the meaning of the equal sign, and determine if equations involving addition and subtraction are true or false. *For example, which of the following equations are true and which are false? 6 = 6, 7 = 8 − 1, 5 + 2 = 2 + 5, 4 + 1 = 5 + 2.*

The picture book *Equal Shmequal* by Virginia Kroll offers a unique way to teach the equal sign. The animals explore equality and fairness using a seesaw and discover that equal numbers and equal sizes are not the same thing. Students may act out this story, or you may assign the animals in the story number values. Using these number values, children can determine what is fair or equal.

After reading this story, use a simple balance scale to demonstrate the concept of the equal sign. You will need the scale, an equal sign, and a set of 20 identical counters (such as bears, dinosaurs, or pennies). Tape an equal sign written on paper to the center point of the balance scale. Tell your class that the scale is a lot like the seesaw in the story. The two sides have to be the same in order for the seesaw to stay even, just like the two sides of the balance scale have to be the same to balance. First, prove that 6 counters on one side and 9 counters on the other side do not balance the scale; one side is lower than the other side. Try a few other combinations that do not balance. Then, demonstrate that 8 counters on one side balance, or equal, the 8 counters on the other side.

Once you have established the function of a balance scale, it is time to count and place 6 identical counters on one side of the balance scale. Ask one child to place a group of 2 counters on the opposite side of the scale. Point out that the scale is not balanced: the side with 6 counters is lower than the empty side. Ask your students how many more counters you would need to place on the opposite side so that both sides equaled 6. Prove that 4 more counters make the scale balanced. Say, "That's right. 6 equals 4 and 2; 4 + 2 = 6." Be sure your students hear you say the statement as a whole and then in two parts, as well as hearing you say the number sentence as part-part-whole.

Identical counters work fine, but, use weighted numbers like the ones shown if you have them—like the animals in the story, weighted numbers are single objects of varying weight.

Pocket Math

 A Pocket for Corduroy by Don Freeman

This classic and popular book is wonderful for counting or adding three whole numbers. Encourage your students to come to school wearing clothing with lots of pockets for this special day. A simple note home or an email blast requesting students come with pockets on this day will add to the fun and increase the numbers.

Each child builds a tower of his Unifix cubes—one for each pocket he is wearing!

- As each child arrives in class, give him one Unifix cube to place in each pocket.

- Place children in groups of three so they have friends to help problem-solve.

- Ask each child to take all Unifix cubes from every pocket and build a tower of cubes to represent their pockets.

- Encourage children to compare their cube towers and say something like, "My tower is shorter than your tower because I have fewer pockets than you." Or "My tower is the tallest tower in our group because I have the most pockets."

- Have each group compute the sum of their three towers.

- When each group reports to the class, have them pose "missing-number" problems for their classmates to solve. For example, if there were 4 cubes for Sam and 5 cubes for Pat and 3 cubes for Joe, they could tell the group that Sam had 4 pockets and Pat had 5 pockets. Then they could give their sum of 12 and ask, "How many pockets did Joe have?"

Math Journal: Have children draw pictures and write a number sentence to show the sum of cubes for their group of three friends.

Extension: As a final wrap-up, you may want to combine all of the groups' Unifix cube towers for a class total of pockets.

 Whole Group, Small Groups

1.OA.D.8 Determine the unknown whole number in an addition or subtraction equation relating three whole numbers. *For example, determine the unknown number that makes the equation true in each of the equations $8 + ? = 11$, $5 = \square - 3$, $6 + 6 = \square$.*

✓ QUICK TIP

If your students are new to this type of "math talk" you will need to model how to talk about the towers. Create a tower for yourself and state several number sentences related to the towers so that your students can hear how you describe them.

◆ C P A ▶

Whole Group, Small Groups, Individuals

2.OA.A.1 Use addition and subtraction within 100 to solve one- and two-step word problems involving situations of adding to, taking from, putting together, taking apart, and comparing, with unknowns in all positions, e.g., by using drawings and equations with a symbol for the unknown number to represent the problem.

GRADE (2)

Cluster 2.OA.A Represent and solve problems involving addition and subtraction.

How Many Critters?

 My Little Sister Ate One Hare by Bill Grossman

My Little Sister Ate One Hare is an outrageously funny book with two key elements of great literature for children: the author mentions both underwear *and* throwing up! The kids will be entranced as you read it aloud. Soon they'll be finishing the lines on each page as you read, showing that they understand the pattern of the story.

To use the book for a math activity, follow steps something like these:

- Read the story to the class, pausing for the laughter that you are sure to hear. (Plan on a few minutes of hysterical laughter when you get to the underwear page.)

- After that first reading, point out that the little sister ate 1 thing, then 2 things, then 3 things, and so on. Then ask, "How many critters did the little sister eat?" Make sure students understand that you are not asking how many of each kind of critter. Say, "It doesn't matter *what* she ate. I'm asking you *how many* she ate."

- Say, "I'm going to give you _____ minutes to solve this problem. Then we'll have a math meeting to compare our answers and our strategies." Give children the freedom to solve this problem using manipulatives, pictures, tally marks, or numbers.

WHATEVER WAY WORKS

As far back as 1825, Warren Colburn wrote that children were successful in mathematics when they were allowed to pursue their own methods rather than being given rules (NAEYC, 2000). I'm thrilled when children tell me how they solved the problems I have posed, and doubly thrilled when other children arrive at the same answer using different methods.

- Add, "If you happen to finish early, remember that good mathematicians *always* check their answers. I'm looking for extra-smart mathematicians who check their work using different strategies."

- Turn them loose to problem-solve. This is your chance to kid-watch, noting who uses cubes, who counts on fingers, and who prefers pictures, tallies, or numbers. Your students' strategies are windows to their understanding; you can use this information as you plan later lessons.

MODELING PROBLEM-SOLVING

As needed, model one problem-solving approach to get students thinking. For example, if no one chose to use a T chart, demonstrate how to do this. Write "Number She Ate" on the left side of a sheet of lined chart paper, write "Total She Ate" on the right side, and then draw a vertical line down the middle of the paper. Go through the story line by line, discussing each line with the class as you add it: "Okay, next she ate 4 disgusting things, so I'll put 4 in the left-hand column. Before she ate those 4, she had already eaten a total of 6 critters, so in the right-hand column I'll put 6 + 4. We know that 6 + 4 = 10 critters total, so I'll put that answer, 10, in the right-hand column, too. Next she ate 5 icky things, so I'll write 5 on the left side. What will I put on the right? That's correct, 10 + 5. " When you are finished, emphasize that this is just <u>one</u> way to solve the problem.

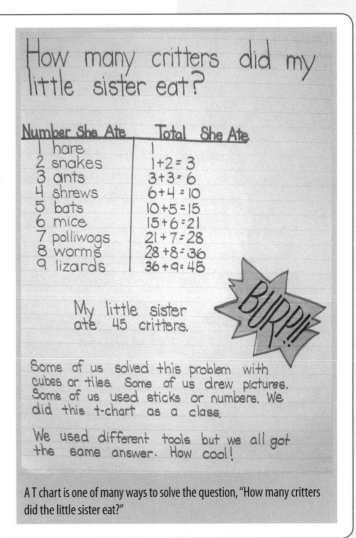

A T chart is one of many ways to solve the question, "How many critters did the little sister eat?"

- When time is up, call children to the math meeting and ask, "How many critters did the little sister eat?"

Give children the freedom to solve problems using any method that works.

- Write down the answers as your students give them. Don't give any facial clues as to whether the answers are correct or not, and don't be concerned if there are some wrong answers. The real learning will come when students explain the different ways they solved the problem to their classmates.

- Ask, "Who would like to justify his or her answer?" Allow students to explain their problem-solving processes. Encourage their classmates to ask questions about why their process worked. Praise innovative thinking and unusual approaches!

- Make sure that several different ways to get the correct answer are presented. Encourage students to ask questions about these approaches.

- Write a summary along these lines to post on a wall: "We read *My Little Sister Ate One Hare*. We figured out how many critters the little sister ate. Some of us used Unifix cubes, some used blocks, some used ducks, some used tallies, some used numbers, and some used T charts. We used different methods, but we all got the same answer."

Variation: Two other good books for this activity are *P. Bear's New Year's Party: A Counting Book* by Paul Owen Lewis and *One Duck Stuck* by Phyllis Root.

Extension: Ask your students how many more disgusting creatures the little sister would have to eat to reach 100 or more. For instance, if she ate 11 cockroaches she would have eaten 56 revolting creatures total. What could she eat 12 of? What would her total be then?

C P A
Whole Group

2.OA.A.1

How Old Is This Class?

Begin by asking, "If we add up the ages of all the children in this class, how old would this class be?" Let children suggest different ways to solve the problem, and then continue along these lines:

- Ask, "How can we discover how old the youngest person in this class is? How can we figure out the age of the oldest person in this class?" (Decide in advance whether adults count as class members!)

- Do a quick survey of the class, asking questions like, "How many of you are 7 years old?"

- Turn this problem over to your little problem solvers, giving them a time frame in which to work. Say something like, "Okay, problem solvers, you have _____ minutes to solve this. You may solve this problem in the way that works best for you. After _____ minutes, we'll have a math meeting to discuss our results. Remember that good mathematicians always check their answers!"

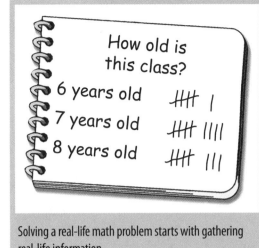

Solving a real-life math problem starts with gathering real-life information.

- Take the opportunity to kid-watch as your class is solving the problem. Observe the different strategies that the children are using.

- After the designated number of minutes, announce, "All right, mathematicians, meet me at the easel and let's discuss how you solved this problem." If you're lucky, your students will have come up with a variety of ways to solve the problem. Celebrate this diversity by asking students to explain their strategies.

- With the children dictating to you as their scribe, write a summary of the activity on chart paper. Use correct mathematical language. You might write something like this: "We added all of our ages and learned that this class is _____ years old! We used cubes, keys, sticks, tallies, and numbers to figure this out."

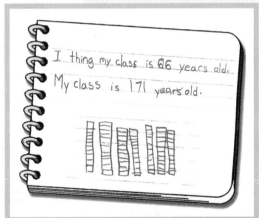

Finding the age of the class makes a great Math Journal entry.

Math Journal: Ask your students to record what they did to solve the problem and what they learned from seeing other people's solutions.

 QUICK TIP

Be sensitive to the makeup of your class. A child who is older or younger than his classmates might end up with hurt feelings. Please consider this before planning an activity that focuses on age.

Candle Count

This is another way to reinforce the idea that many different approaches can all lead to the same answer.

- Begin by asking, "How many birthday candles have you blown out in your lifetime? That's kind of a tough problem to solve. So before we call out numbers, let's think of some organized ways to solve this problem."

- Say, "Let's think about this. When you were 1, you blew out 1 candle. When you were 2, you blew out 2 candles. When you were 3, you blew out _____." Let children fill in the answer of 3 candles. "Does anyone see a pattern here?"

- Once students see the pattern, introduce the problem: "I want you to figure out how many candles you have blown out in your lifetime. You can use any method you'd like. Once you've solved this problem, prove your answer. We'll have a math meeting in _____ minutes and we can discuss the answer then."

- Send the candle-blowers off to solve the problem, and then gather them into a group at the designated time.

This child figured out his candle count by writing the abstract numbers in an organized way.

Pictures are a wonderful way for a student to organize her thinking while problem-solving.

• Ask, "Will everyone in this classroom have the same answer? Why? Or why not?" Some children may mention differences in family traditions, such as adding a candle to grow on or having more than one celebration. It's up to you whether your students should consider these candles in their counts.

• Allow discussion of the different numbers of candles that have been blown out and why the numbers are different.

• Take time to celebrate the fact that there are many ways to solve this problem. Let your students know that you are proud of them for thinking of different ways to figure out the candle count.

Making a chart of dots, one dot for each candle, is a good way to solve the candle count problem.

GRADE 2

Cluster 2.OA.B Add and subtract within 20.

2.OA.B.2 Fluently add and subtract within 20 using mental strategies. By end of Grade 2, know from memory all sums of two one-digit numbers.

Panda Poop

 Panda Math by Ann Whitehead Nagda

Ann has done it again with this nonfiction book about a little panda growing up in a zoo. Enjoy this book as a read-aloud, and then spend some time using the examples to practice math skills. For example, compensation with subtraction is a strategy used on pages 20 to 25. We especially like "Poo's Clues" on page 20. It may sound outrageous to adults, but the topic of panda poop is very engaging to primary students! This task engages students as they help the zookeepers find the difference in the number of poop piles found at night as opposed to the number of piles found in the daytime.

SEE WHAT THEY KNOW

This rich, open-ended task will show you how comfortable your second graders are with manipulating numbers. Choose the format that works best for observing how your students approach solving the problem: whole class or small groups with teacher support, or independent. This problem is available as a copymaster on page 169 in case you'd like to give your students a copy to follow along with. Provide paper, rulers, scissors, cubes, and any other materials that may help them prove to themselves that Judd is correct, and to explain how they know he is correct.

"John has cut two strips of paper. One strip is 12 inches long and the other strip is 10 inches long. Judd says that he can cut 1 inch off of each strip, and the two strips will still have a difference of 2 inches. John does not believe this. He thinks that cutting off 2 inches will make one strip 4 inches longer than the other. Who is right, and why is he right? Use pictures, equations, and words to prove your answer. You may also use Unifix cubes, rulers, or any other classroom materials to show your work."

GRADE ②

Cluster 2.OA.C Work with equal groups of objects to gain foundations for multiplication.

Odd & Even Names

 Chrysanthemum by Kevin Henkes

In this book, a mouse learns to love her 13-letter name in spite of her classmates' taunts. This activity provides an opportunity for your students to use their own names to explore odd and even numbers and to investigate what happens when we add these kinds of numbers. Record a list of each child's first name in your class on 1-inch gridded easel paper. Use red for names that have an odd number of letters. Use blue for names that have an even number of letters.

Next, count the letters in each name by 2s until the class discovers what red and blue stand for. Then, have students find partners and add together the number of letters in both of their first names. Record the results where everyone can see them, with the even sums written in blue and the odd sums written in red.

Ask questions to encourage students to see the patterns in the sums. "Do 2 red names (odds) equal an odd sum or an even sum? What about 2 blue names (evens)? What happens when you add a blue (even) and a red (odd)? Are these patterns true for the sums of other names?"

Whole Group, Pairs

2.OA.C.3 Determine whether a group of objects (up to 20) has an odd or even number of members, e.g., by pairing objects or counting them by 2s; write an equation to express an even number as a sum of two equal addends.

Array's a Way!

Demonstrate an array of 12 square Cheez-It crackers (or another snack or square plastic tiles) using an interactive whiteboard or document camera, or on the floor with the children grouped around you. Explain that arrays are rectangles. In an array, all rows have an equal number of objects. Point out that an array of 12 with 4 rows of 3 is the same as $3 + 3 + 3 + 3 = 12$. Write out this number sentence so that the children see the symbolic connection to the manipulatives. Point out that a single horizontal line is an array of 1 row of 12. A single vertical line is an array of 12 rows of 1.

Provide each student with a set of 8 Cheez-Its or square tiles. Ask, "How many different ways can you arrange 8 Cheez-Its (tiles)?" Instruct each child to lay her 8 crackers on a piece of paper and then

Whole Group, Individuals

2.OA.C.4 Use addition to find the total number of objects arranged in rectangular arrays with up to 5 rows and up to 5 columns; write an equation to express the total as a sum of equal addends.

trace around them. Encourage children to create a variety of shapes using their 8 crackers.

After they have had experience with 8 objects, make the task a bit more complex. Hand each student 4 more objects and ask, "How many arrays can you make using 12 squares? With 8 squares, we made any kind of shape. This time let's make just arrays." Students trace around their objects, as they did before. Encourage students to share their array solutions. Choose several examples, and write the repeated addition number sentence that each array represents.

> ## ✓ QUICK TIP
>
> *A child might make an array of 2 × 4 or 4 × 2, but he may also make an L, a U, and so on. That's okay. Even though you are working on arrays right now, seeing that 8 crackers can be arranged in a variety of ways builds the foundation for discussing the concept of area. Do, however, ask students to identify which of the arrangements are arrays and which are not and to explain how they know.*

Whole Group

2.OA.C.4

Array a Day

This activity builds day by day. Each day, you and your students will make one card that shows all possible arrays for one number. Decide in advance what number you're working up to. For each day, you'll need a 12-inch square of black paper mounted on a 13-inch square of red or blue to create a colored border; you'll need half red and half blue borders. You will also need a variety of small, lightweight objects or stickers, and crayons or markers that are made to write on black construction paper.

The first day, hang a black square with a red border where all the children can see it. Explain that you'll be making number cards to display, one each day. Today you are starting with the number 1. Draw a 1 in the corner of the black square. Describe what you are doing as you are making the card. Glue one large thing to the card, such as a picture or lightweight item. Say, "One is an odd number." Write "One is odd." at the bottom of the card.

Give each odd number a red frame. Give each even number a blue frame.

On the second day, write a 2 in the corner of a black square mounted on blue. Say, "Today's square is on blue, and yesterday's square was on red. Why do you think I've done this?" Elicit ideas, and praise all predictions. Tell students they'll have to wait until more cards are up to see if they're correct.

Review or define the idea of an array. Show students the objects you are planning to use with the 2 card—for example, feathers. Ask, "How many different ways can I arrange these feathers to make arrays for 2?" Survey the class for answers, and then confirm: "Yes, you're correct. I can arrange 2 feathers in 1 horizontal row or in 1 vertical row." Have some students help you glue 4 feathers into the 2 arrays (1 horizontal and 1 vertical).

When the students are finished, circle each array. As you do so, say, "This array is 1 horizontal line, so I'm going to write below it, '1 set of 2 equals 2.'" For the vertical line, say "This array is 2 sets of 1, so I'm going to write that '2 sets of 1 equals 2.' This card also shows 1 plus 1, so I'll write that, too." Write 1 + 1 = 2.

The next day, make a 3 card with a red border. Talk students through thinking about the number of arrays: 1 set of 3 arranged horizontally, and 3 sets of 1 arranged vertically. Let students help with the objects, circle the arrays, and add the math statements to the card, explaining as you go.

Continue each day with the next number. As numbers get larger, some will have more arrays. Encourage students to identify all of the arrays for a number, writing them on the board to keep track. For example, the number 12 will have 6 arrays: 12 × 1, 1 × 12, 6 × 2, 2 × 6, 4 × 3, and 3 × 4. When all possible arrays have been named, plan with the class how to arrange them on the card. Make sure to leave room for the math sentences—remember, you need to circle each array, such as 4 rows of 3, and say, "This is 3 plus 3 plus 3 plus 3 equals 12."

Continue making cards day after day until you reach the number you desire for your class.

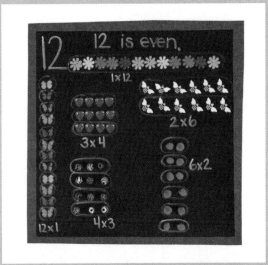

You'll need to use smaller items with numbers like 12, 16, and 18, since there are so many arrays that can be made for those numbers. Sequins, stickers, or small beads work well.

*Whole Group,
Individuals*

2.OA.C.4

Hungry Kitty

Six-Dinner Sid by Inga Moore

This is the tale of Sid, a unique cat who lives at 6 different houses, has 6 different names, and eats 6 different dinners each night. Streets named after famous mathematicians provide a backdrop for multiple math tasks. Younger children love to count the 6 meals, while your second graders can use a 6×7 array to pictorially compute how many dinners Sid the Cat would eat in one week. This activity calls for an array with one more row and two more columns than the standard requires, but your children should be able to manage it!

Number and Operations in Base Ten

We are certain of one thing in math education: it is impossible to spend too much time on place value. Experts believe that the Hindu people of India first developed, about 1,000 years ago, the base-10 number system as we understand it today. Arab people who traded with the Hindus adopted the number system and improved upon it. A critical piece of this system was the 0. Its use as a placeholder and number makes our system easier to learn and to use than many earlier systems. If it were not for those mathematicians who saw the beauty in 0 and base 10, we might still be adding and subtracting with the Roman numerals I, V, X, L, and C.

According to the Common Core State Standards, our kindergartners are expected to understand numbers from 11 to 19 as a set of ten and ones. Our first graders should be able to use mental math to add and subtract multiples of 10 within 100. Second graders are expected to understand numbers to 1,000; fluently add and subtract within 100; and add and subtract within 1,000, using a variety of strategies.

In the three years from kindergarten to grade 2, we are building the critical foundation for numbers to the millions and beyond, as well as for decimals and percentages. This is serious stuff, and we have to take it seriously—even when taking it seriously means dressing a child like the superhero Zero! Like we said, it is impossible to spend too much time on place value!

Our number system is based on 10!

K.NBT.A.1 Compose
and decompose numbers
from 11 to 19 into ten
ones and some further
ones, e.g., by using objects
or drawings, and record
each composition or
decomposition by a
drawing or equation (e.g.,
18 = 10 + 8); understand
that these numbers are
composed of ten ones and
one, two, three, four, five,
six, seven, eight, or nine
ones.

GRADE Ⓚ

Cluster K.NBT.A Work with numbers 11–19 to gain foundations for place value.

Giant Double Ten-Frame

Make a giant-size double 10-frame using colored tape on a dollar-store shower curtain, or draw one on bulletin board paper. Get some colorful plastic party cups or plates to use as counters.

Use the giant double 10-frame to model the expression 10 + 2. Place 10 party cups in the first 10-frame and 2 party cups in the second 10-frame. This will show students that there is 1 set of 10 and 2 ones in 12. But wait until later to write the numbers.

- Tell the children, "We have a full 10-frame here, right? So how many cups do we have in this frame?" (Let kids come up with their reasons for answering "10.")

- Model how to count on from 10 for the total of 10 + 2: "We have 10 cups here. I am trying to figure out how many cups there are in

A giant double 10-frame is great for showing numbers between 11 and 20. This double 10-frame shows that 12 is 10 and 2 more.

all. Let's all say '10' for the first 10-frame, and then let's count on from 10 for the cups in the second 10-frame. Ready? 10" (pointing to the cups in the full frame), "11" (touching the first cup in the second frame), "12" (touching the second cup in the second frame).

• Let kids digest this very important concept and then ask, "What just happened? Why didn't we have to count all of the cups in the first frame?" Let students give some ideas, and then explain. "See, we're smart mathematicians. We know we do not have to count all 10 cups. We know there are 10 because the 10-frame is full. So we counted 10, and then we counted on from 10 for the other 2 cups, and we got to 12."

• Again, this is such an important concept. Let your students mull this over. You may want to repeat this example several times before continuing on with the abstract symbols for this number sentence.

• Prepare two index cards: one with the number 10 written on it in red, and another with the number 2 on it in blue. Write the number sentence 10 + 2 = 12 where all students can see it.

• Say, "Boys and girls, this number sentence is just what we did with our cups. There were 10 cups and 2 more cups, and we had 12 cups in all."

• Show the card with 10 written in red on it. Place the 2 card over the 0 in the number 10. "Look closely at this total, 12. Do you see the 10 here?" (Pull the cards apart.) "That 1 means 1 set of 10, like the set of cups. Do you see the 2? That means 2 more, 2 ones, just like the set of 2 cups." (Place the 10 and 2 together to form 12.)

• Make blue cards for the other numerals so you can show students that this works for other numbers and number sentences.

Math Journal: Ask students to draw what they just did with the party cups and the 10-frames. Have them draw 10 stars and circle the 10, then draw "and 2 more."

Extension: Extend this very powerful lesson with, "Who can show me 10 + 5 using the cups?" Keep doing this as long as there is interest. Once the eyes start to roll and the bodies start wiggling, move on. Bring it out again for several days in a row for small potent doses!

 QUICK TIP

You can also demonstrate one connected set of 10 and unattached ones using Unifix cubes, links, or snap blocks. Each time you show the concrete materials using two colors, you are reinforcing this concept as well as connecting the abstract to the concrete.

Ten in a Row +

Glue small cutouts, stickers, or stamps in two rows on a strip of card stock. Put 10 shapes in the top row and fewer than 10 shapes in the bottom row, taking care to line up the shapes in the bottom row below the shapes in the top row. Then talk about the rows of shapes using reasoning along these lines:

"There are 10 fish in the top row. So how many fish are there in all? You already know the top row has 10. See, you do not have to count all of the shapes to find the answer." You want your students to think, "Hmm . . . I know there are 10 fish on the top, so I don't need to count them! And I see another 4 fish, so that means 10 and 4 more. Ten and 4 more is 14."

When your students see two rows totaling 18 fish, you want them to think, "Hmm . . . there are 10 fish on the top row, and the next row is missing 2 fish, so there must be 8 fish in the second row. Ten fish and 8 fish make 18 fish. That means 10 + 8 = 18."

Each strip is 12 inches by 4 inches. Cutouts in a contrasting color stand out well, so the children can easily see and count each shape—or see and know the number without counting.

After you have introduced the strips to the class and they understand the format, this is a great way to fill the extra few minutes while you wait for the buses or for a school visitor. Watch your students turn it into a game on their own!

Variation: Individually flash the 10 in a Row + strips to each child. Can she tell the total number of shapes without counting the top row?

Extension: Once your children understand the concept of counting by 10s, increase the number of cutouts to give them practice with 20 +, 30 +, and so forth.

QUICK TIP

These strips do a great job of reinforcing 10 + for all sums less than 20—you'll want to make a 10 + strip for each of the numbers 1 through 9. Once you have introduced the concept of 10 + 1, 10 + 2, and so on, you'll find yourself pulling out these strips all year long. You'll also find your mathematicians computing answers more fluently.

SEE WHAT THEY KNOW

Choose the format that works best for observing your students: one-on-one or small groups. Show 10 Unifix cubes snapped together and a few more Unifix cubes (fewer than 10) that are not snapped together. Say, "There are 10 cubes in this tower. How many cubes are there in all?" Point to all of the cubes. Note whether the child counts on from 10. If there were 6 cubes in addition to the tower of 10, does he see and say the addition sentence 10 + 6 = 16?

Counting School Days

This year long activity is easy to implement and provides your students with a daily dose of place value. It also builds their sense of tens and ones beyond the number 19. Begin with 18 blank 10-frames mounted on one poster. Place 1 sticker in a 10-frame each day. If you have 180 school days, then all 18 10-frames will be complete on the last day of school. If you have a different number of days, adjust accordingly the number of 10-frames used. Whenever a 10-frame is filled, celebrate by choosing a child to be "Zero the Hero" for the day. You can even make a cape like the one shown on page 71.

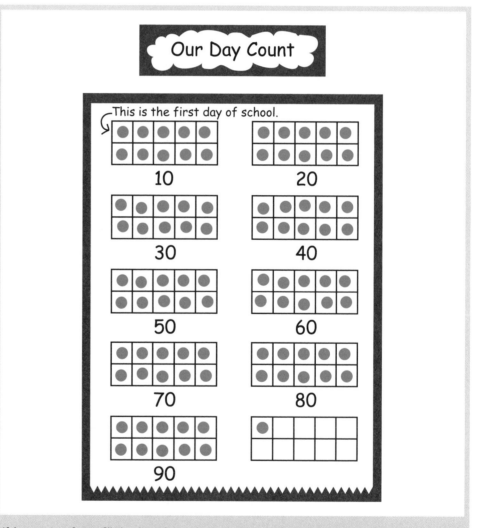

If there are 9 10-frames filled and 1 sticker on the tenth 10-frame, then it is Day 91 of school. Day 91 has 9 sets of 10 stickers (9 tens) and 1 single sticker (1 one). Pages 71 and 72 show some other ways to count the days of school by tens.

GRADE ①

Cluster 1.NBT.A Extend the counting sequence.

Number Line

Start this activity early in the school year and plan enough space to continue it all year long! Hang the beginning of a number line in your room, using adding machine tape or colored sentence strips. Each day, write one number on the number line. Every 10 days, change to a different colored marker or start a different colored sentence strip so the decades stand out. Each time the count reaches 10, 20, 30, 40, and so on, highlight that number with glitter, a smile in the 0, or a star.

Variation: If you prefer, you can create the number line from cutouts that are consistent in shape and color for each group of 10—for example, numbers 1 to 10 on red triangles, numbers 11 to 20 on pink circles, numbers 21 to 30 on orange squares, and so forth.

Whole Group

1.NBT.A.1 Count to 120, starting at any number less than 120. In this range, read and write numerals and represent a number of objects with a written numeral.

Estimate Jar

Use a large, clear plastic jar, the kind that bulk pretzels or candy comes in. Place a large number of identical items into the jar, such as dry lima beans, marbles, pom-poms, or animal crackers. Make sure to use a multiple of 10 items, such as 30, 40, or 50. Ask kids to estimate the number of items in the jar. This is a great activity for Monday through Thursday. Let them change their estimates based on new information—that's an important life skill. On Friday, assemble everyone so you can discuss the range of estimates. Who has the highest estimate? Who has the estimate closest to 0?

Next, spill the contents of the jar—let's say pom-poms—onto the floor or table. Spread out the pom-poms so that each one can be seen. Ask children if they want to change their estimates. Don't rush this process; give your scholars time to consider their original estimates. Once all estimates are in, carefully count 10 pom-poms, encouraging the children to count with you. As you count, place each pom-pom on a paper plate that is labeled 10. Once you have modeled this, ask

Whole Group, Individuals

1.NBT.A.1

An array is one organized way to count the items from the estimate jar, after all students have made their estimates. Another is to count out sets of 10 onto paper plates.

Fill the jar with a multiple of 10 items, and let children make estimates all week before counting on Friday. Let them change their estimates based on new information—that's an important life skill.

for a volunteer to count out 10 more pom-poms and place those on a second paper plate labeled 10. Once all of the pom-poms have been counted onto plates, say, "Now let's count by 10s." Point to each plate in turn, saying, "10, 20, 30 . . . ."

Do this each week using different multiples of 10 objects, and with objects of different sizes, until your students get the hang of counting by 10s. Then, instead of labeling each paper plate 10, label the plates 10, 20, 30, 40, 50, and on up to 100 (or however many objects you are using that week). As the 10 plate is filled, fill the 20 plate. As the 20 plate is filled, fill the 30 plate. This repeated practice will build strong understanding of how to count by 10s, and will demonstrate that counting by 10s saves time.

Extension: Any time you have items to count, like the pumpkin seeds in the class pumpkin or the buttons in the button box, always count in sets of 10. Place all counters on paper and circle each set of 10, or place sets of 10 on paper plates or in cupcake wrappers so the children see these as equal sets of 10. Be consistent when it comes to counting large quantities by using this strategy, and your students will truly build their understanding of tens and ones place value.

GRADE 1

Cluster 1.NBT.B Understand place value.

Daily Count

Whole Group

Your class can enjoy this activity for the whole school year. Set aside a special place that's easy for everyone to see. Find or make a set of pockets like the ones shown, or use small boxes or cans. Each day of the school year, add a straw to the ones pocket (or box or can). Tell students that only 9 straws can fit in the ones pocket (or that only 9 are allowed in it), so on the tenth day, bundle the straws together and place the bundle in the tens pocket. On the hundredth day of school, bundle up the 10 sets of straws and place them in the hundreds pocket. So for example, on Day 163 there should be 1 bundle of 100 straws (10 sets of 10) in the hundreds pocket, 6 bundles of 10 straws in the tens pocket, and 3 single straws in the ones pocket. Every tenth day, when the straws in the ones pocket are bundled and placed in the tens pocket, celebrate by choosing a boy or girl to be "Zero the Hero"! You can make a cape like the one shown below for your hero to wear.

> **1.NBT.B.2a**
> Understand that the two digits of a two-digit number represent amounts of tens and ones. Understand the following as a special case: 10 can be thought of as a bundle of ten ones—called a "ten."

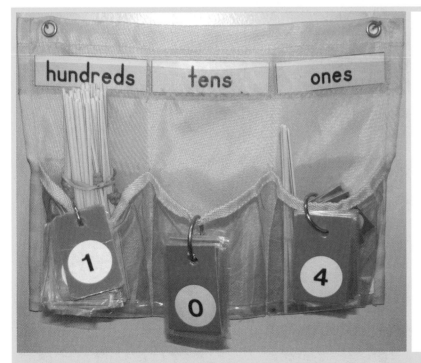

Day 104 looks like this when you count the days of school with straws. Whenever 10 straws are bundled, celebrate by choosing a child to wear a special "Zero the Hero" cape for the day! Pages 68 and 72 show some other ways to count the days of school by tens.

Chains of Ten

Another way to reinforce the crucial benchmark of 10 throughout the school year is with chains of 10. The chains can be constructed from paper, paper clips, or plastic links. Each day of school, add a link to the chain. Once you have a chain that's 10 links long, hang it where the class can see it; then begin another chain. For example, on Day 57 of school, the children will see 5 separate complete chains of 10 and another chain with only 7 links. When you have 10 chains of 10, connect them into 1 chain of 100.

Day 57 of school: Five children hold chains of 10; the sixth holds a chain of 7. Pages 68 and 71 show some other ways to count the days of school by tens.

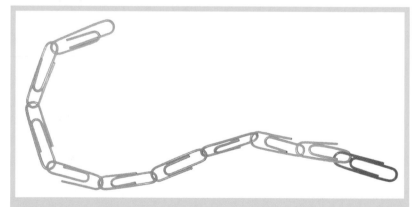

Placing a different colored clip on the end of a chain of 10 helps makes the 10s stand out when you connect 10 chains of 10 into one chain of 100 on the 100th day of school.

Counting by Feet

 One Is a Snail, Ten Is a Crab: A Counting by Feet Book by April Pulley Sayre and Jeff Sayre

After reading April Pulley Sayre and Jeff Sayre's book *One Is a Snail, Ten Is a Crab: A Counting by Feet Book,* your students will understand that the 10 feet on a crab plus the 2 feet on a person equals 12 feet in all. (Yes, 10 crab feet; read the book for scientific details.) And they'll understand that the 10 feet on a crab plus the 8 feet on a spider equals 18 feet.

After enjoying the book as a class, ask your students to create number sentences for the number of feet for one crab and one other creature of their own choosing. Some of your students may also want to stretch themselves by adding the feet from two other creatures to the crab foot count.

Math Journal: Have students write their number sentences in their journals and then show their artistic sides by drawing the creatures whose feet they are adding.

C P A

Whole Group, Individuals

1.NBT.B.2b
Understand that the two digits of a two-digit number represent amounts of tens and ones. Understand the following as a special case: The numbers from 11 to 19 are composed of a ten and one, two, three, four, five, six, seven, eight, or nine ones.

18 is a lobster and octopus.

Jacob Holtman   18.

19 is a lobster, octopus and sea snail.

Allison Yang   19.

Students can extend the story by adding the feet of more than one sea creature.

*Whole Group, Small
Groups, Individuals*

1.NBT.B.2c
Understand that the two
digits of a two-digit
number represent
amounts of tens and ones.
Understand the following
as a special case: The numbers 10, 20, 30, 40, 50, 60,
70, 80, 90 refer to one,
two, three, four, five, six,
seven, eight, or nine tens
(and 0 ones).

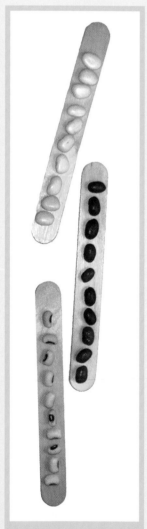

Three completed bean sticks,
each with 10 beans

Bean Sticks

A bean stick is a craft stick that has 10 lima beans, garbanzo beans, or other beans of a similar size glued to it. These tried-and-true sticks are a popular and effective way to help students understand the base-10 system.

Begin by having each child make 10 bean sticks. (Do not be tempted to ask a parent or aide to do this. The children need to do it themselves so that they *really believe* there are 10 beans on each stick.)

Here's how to make and use bean sticks:

- Give 10 craft sticks to each child. Have the child write her name in pencil on one side of each stick, and then turn the sticks over.

- Using a paper plate as a work mat, the child pours a generous amount of glue from one end of a stick to the other. This is one time you don't have to say, "Not too much glue, please."

- The child places 10 beans into the glue on the stick, and then repeats the process for each of her other sticks.

- Leave the paper plates with the bean sticks to dry overnight.

- After the glue has dried completely, you can start the bean stick lessons. Start by saying, "There are 10 beans on each stick. We don't have to count the beans since you know you already counted them, right?" (Children should agree.)

- Say, "Show me 10 beans." (Each child pulls out 1 stick.)

- Say, "Show me 20 beans." (Each child pulls out 2 sticks.)

- Continue to do this until children are sure that each stick rep-resents 10.

- Next, give each child a cup containing 10 individual beans.

- Say, "Show me 12 beans." (Children should show 1 stick and 2 loose beans.)

- Ask, "Why is this a better way to show 12 than using 12 loose beans?" (Children should understand that having a set of 10 makes it quicker and easier to show 12 because you just have to count out 2 more beans to add to 1 stick of 10 beans.)

- Continue this process for 24, 54, and 35, reinforcing the concept, for example, that 35 is 3 sticks and 5 loose beans.

Don't rush it—do bean stick lessons over the course of many days. Some days you will accomplish only one or two steps. That's okay. Consistency pays off! The students *will* get it. Mastering place value takes time—and constant reinforcement.

PROPORTIONALITY AND PLACE VALUE

Bean sticks make great manipulatives for base 10 because they are proportional: the beans fill the stick, so the stick is 10 times the size of 1 bean. Working from the concrete to the symbolic helps students develop an understanding of proportionality that's critical for developing place-value knowledge (Van de Walle et. al., 2003). The value of 10 compared with the value of 1 is clear and concrete on a bean stick!

Tens-and-Ones Mats

This activity takes bean sticks to the pictorial level. Give a sheet of construction paper to each child. Have children follow along as you fold the paper in half lengthwise, draw a line along the fold, and write the labels "tens" and "ones" at the top, as shown in the photo. Then name some numbers between 10 and 100 for children to show on their mats, using their bean sticks. Turn to page 79 for another bean stick activity.

Whole Group

1.NBT.B.2c

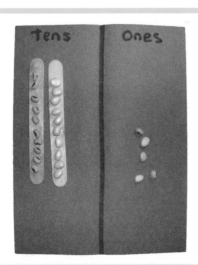

Say, "When I ask you to show 25, please put 2 bean sticks on the tens side and 5 loose beans on the ones side." Practice this *many* times with many different numbers.

Cereal Count

Give each pair or small group of children a paper plate or sheet of construction paper to be the "counting plate," and several soufflé cups or cupcake papers. To each plate, add a scoop of cold cereal similar to Cheerios or Fruit Loops. (We like to use the most inexpensive generic cereal available.) Caution the children not to "eat the math," as other people will handle the cereal later.

Ask the children to guess how many cereal pieces they have and to share that guess with their partners. Once they have guessed, they may start counting. Say, "Mathematicians, this looks like a big pile of cereal, but all you need to do is count to 10! Once you've counted 10 cereal pieces, place those 10 pieces in a cup and start counting again. Each time you've counted 10 pieces, start another cup of 10." This process is not as easy as it sounds; sometimes cereal pieces get stuck to fingers and cereal needs to be recounted.

As pairs start to finish up, say, "Once all of your pieces are counted, line up your cups of 10 and count by 10s." If there are leftover pieces, have children count on from the highest multiple of ten, or have them mentally add the leftover pieces. If this is too confusing, ask them to turn the extra pieces back to you.

Children can count to any number, no matter how great, as long as they can count to 10!

Antler Points Count

This lesson is a December favorite! Have children make simple reindeer by rolling 12 × 18-inch sheets of brown construction paper into cones, stapling them, and adding paper eyes and noses. For the math connection, children add the antler points. Have them trace around their hands onto construction paper and glue the cutout hands to the top of each cone. All finished reindeer have 10 antler points.

Call groups of children to the front of the room with their completed reindeer. Count the number of noses by 1s, eyes by 2s, and points by 10s!

After lots of counting, mount the reindeer on the wall to make a fantastic seasonal bulletin board.

*Whole Group,
Small Groups*

1.NBT.B.3 Compare two two-digit numbers based on meanings of the tens and ones digits, recording the results of comparisons with the symbols >, =, and <.

What's More?

In first grade, most students can confidently compare quantities of objects and say which is more. But comparing written numbers is very abstract, and it takes a lot of practice to master it. Here are some ways to provide that all-important practice.

First make sure that your students understand what it means to compare two numbers. Ask them if they'd rather have 100 gold pieces or 30 gold pieces, and to explain why. Then write the number sentence 100 > 30 and say, "The symbol is like an arrow. The arrow always points to the number that is less. One hundred is more than 30." Next, write the number sentence 30 < 100 and say, "30 is less than 100. The arrow is pointing the other way because it always points to the number that is less."

Provide lots of practice comparing two-digit numbers.

- Display numbers using a document camera or interactive whiteboard, and ask your students to put the correct symbol in between the numbers.

- Point out that the hundred chart and the number line are helpful tools for comparing two different numbers. Remind children that the number closer to 0 is always less than the number farther from 0, on both the number line and the hundred chart.

- Write the symbol < on a paper plate. Write two numbers on a board (for example, 63 and 75), leaving a space between them large enough to accommodate the paper plate. Hand the plate to a student, and ask him to hold the plate between the two numbers so that the arrow faces the number that is the lesser of the two.

 QUICK TIP

Keep practicing! Do not expect your class to master comparing written numbers in one day or even two. Then, when students have mastered the concept, review and practice it from time to time.

GRADE 1

Cluster 1.NBT.C Use place value understanding and properties of operations to add and subtract.

Building on Bean Sticks

Once students have mastered the basic concept of tens and ones, it's time to build on that knowledge. Make sure every student has his bean sticks, his loose beans, and his tens-and-ones mat from the bean sticks activities on pages 74 and 75. Review how to use bean sticks if it's been a while. Then proceed along these lines:

- Say, "Show 63." (Make sure everyone has done this correctly, placing 6 bean sticks on the left side of the mat and 3 loose beans on the right.)

- Say, "Add 10 more." Each child should add 1 more bean stick.

- Say, "Let's count. Point to your bean sticks and beans as we count. Start with the tens." (With you leading, students should count, "10, 20, 30, 40, 50, 60, 70, 71, 72, 73.")

- As children gain understanding, ask them to add 20, 30, and so on to the number you start with.

- Once children have mastered adding 10s to their bean stick numbers, ask them to add 24, 32, and similar numbers.

Be prepared to see amazing results from your students!

Find It! Addition

For each child, you'll need 1 clear, colored chip and 1 copy of a hundred chart. (Find a hundred chart online.) It helps to display a hundred chart on your document camera or interactive whiteboard as well. That way you can move a chip on the board as the children move the chips on their game boards.

Go *very slowly* through the steps. This is a good 10- to 15-minute activity to supplement a lesson. Children will need lots of repeated practice over several days with each step, and some steps may need to be broken into more than one lesson or even spread out over more than one week. The process goes like this:

Whole Group

1.NBT.C.4 Add within 100, including adding a two-digit number and a one-digit number, and adding a two-digit number and a multiple of 10, using concrete models or drawings and strategies based on place value, properties of operations, and/or the relationship between addition and subtraction; relate the strategy to a written method and explain the reasoning used. Understand that in adding two-digit numbers, one adds tens and tens, ones and ones; and sometimes it is necessary to compose a ten.

Whole Group

1.NBT.C.5 Given a two-digit number, mentally find 10 more or 10 less than the number, without having to count; explain the reasoning used.

100 Chart Game Board

1	2	3	4	5	6	7	8	9	10
11	12	13	14	15	16	17	18	19	20
21	22	23	24	25	26	27	28	29	30
31	32	33	34	35	36	37	38	39	40
41	42	43	44	45	46	47	48	49	50
51	52	53	54	55	56	57	58	59	60
61	62	63	64	65	66	67	68	69	70
71	72	73	74	75	76	77	78	79	80
81	82	83	84	85	86	87	88	89	90
91	92	93	94	95	96	97	98	99	100

Finding 25 to place the red chip is, by itself, a task for the young child; model it on your hundred chart. Make sure all of your students have found the starting number before adding tens and ones to it.

- Hand out a plain hundred chart and a colored chip to each child.

- Say, "Place your disk on 25."

- Say, "After you place your disk on 25, add 1, and then add 1 again. Where are you?" Model this for students.

- Practice this a few times starting at different numbers.

- When children are comfortable adding 1s, start adding 10s. Say, "Place your disk on 45, and then add 10." This is your time for a little drama as you move your chip 10 times on your own hundred chart. Say, "Where are you now? *Wow!* There has to be an easier way to move this many spaces! What did you notice happening when I moved 10 spaces?" You may have to guide students by pointing out where your chip was and where it is now. You hope someone will see that adding 10 means dropping the chip to the space directly below where it was originally on the hundred chart.

- Say, "Look! The number in the ones place in 45 is 5, and the number in the ones place in 55 is also 5. Why do you think that is?" Encourage discussion and observations. Point out the similar patterns throughout the chart.

- Continue by saying, "What do you notice about the numbers in the tens place each time we add 10?" It is important that the

QUICK TIP

Encourage your students to use the hundred charts in the classroom. This is a valuable and easily accessible tool that helps children see the patterns in the number system. Post them everywhere that your children might see them—even in the bathroom!

children see that each time 10 is added, the number in the ones place stays the same, and the number in the tens place increases by 1.

- Say, "Whenever we want to add 10, we drop to the number below. Let's practice that. Start at 67 and add 10." Practice adding 10 to several numbers before moving on.

- Next ask, "How would I add 20?" Discuss this with the class, and then practice with a few different numbers.

Extension: Try more complicated additions. Say "Place your disk on 63. Add 10; add 5; add 20. Where are you?" When students have mastered this with the chip, say, "Hands behind your back. Start at 28; add 10; add 10; add 2. Where are you?" Encourage children to come up with their own directions for finding the correct position on the hundred chart.

Find It! Subtraction

Whole Group

This is just like Find It! Addition (above), but you use the hundred chart to subtract numbers instead of adding. Begin by subtracting 10, and discuss what happens when 10 is subtracted. Lead students to discover that, when 10 is subtracted, the ones place has the same number and the tens place is 1 less than the original number. Work through subtracting 10, 20, and so forth. Practice, practice, practice!

1.NBT.C.6 Subtract multiples of 10 in the range 10–90 from multiples of 10 in the range 10–90 (positive or zero differences), using concrete models or drawings and strategies based on place value, properties of operations, and/or the relationship between addition and subtraction; relate the strategy to a written method and explain the reasoning used.

 SEE WHAT THEY KNOW

Here's a question you can use to uncover your students' thinking processes. Let them use hundred charts if you like.

"Cade says that he can find the difference between 41 and 14 by taking away 10, then taking away 1, and finally taking away 3 to get 27. Can you explain his thinking? Did he attend to precision?"

You're looking to see that they understand that Cade first decomposed 14 into 10 and 4 and then took 10 from 41, leaving 31. Then he decomposed the 4 into 1 and 3 and took away 1, leaving 30. That left 3 to take away from 30, taking him to 27.

**Whole Group, Small
Groups, Individuals**

2.NBT.A.1a
Understand that the three
digits of a three-digit
number represent
amounts of hundreds,
tens, and ones; e.g., 706
equals 7 hundreds, 0 tens,
and 6 ones. Understand
the following as a special
case: 100 can be thought
of as a bundle of ten
tens—called a "hundred."

GRADE ②

Cluster 2.NBT.A Understand place value.

Counting Shoes and Socks

Centipede's 100 Shoes by Tony Ross

For this lesson on place value to 142, you'll need 71 straws cut in half (for a total of 142 pieces), rubber bands for bundling, and a large place-value mat showing ones, tens, and hundreds, in addition to the storybook. Children need crayons and their own personal place-value mats that they can write on.

Read *Centipede's 100 Shoes* by Tony Ross to the class. This precious story lends legs to place value and to the task of counting. A centipede buys 100 shoes thinking that he has 100 legs, since that is the meaning of his name. But he soon finds out that he, like most centipedes, has only 42 legs—so he doesn't even need 58 of his shoes! When the shoes hurt his feet, he knows that 42 socks will do the job. After several days of taking off and putting on so many socks and shoes, he decides to give all 100 shoes and 42 socks to friends with fewer legs. Lead a class exploration of the book's mathematics:

- Say, "We are going to use short straws to represent little centipede's socks and shoes on the large place-value mat." (Use one of the half-straws to represent each shoe and one for each sock.)

- Say, "We are going to represent the 100 shoes and the 42 socks that little centipede has decided to give away." (Place straws one by one into the ones place until you have 10.)

- Say, "Since we are working in base 10, we have to regroup our ones into a bundle of 10 and move the 1 bundle to the tens place." (Use a rubber band to bundle the 10 half-straws, and then move the bundle to the tens place on the place-value mat.)

- After moving the first bundle of 10, add more straws one by one until you make a second bundle of 10. Continue until the class has placed 10 bundles of 10 half-straws on the class mat in the tens place. Then say, "We can't have 10 of anything in one place value. We had to turn 10 straws into 1 bundle and move it to the tens

QUICK TIP

We like to have 10 teams of children each make a bundle of 10 half-straws and bring them to the large place-value mat.

place, every time we had 10 straws. Now we have 10 bundles in the tens place. What can we do?"

- Give children time to think and answer, and then say, "Yes, let's bundle the 10 bundles of 10 straws. That makes 1 bundle of 100 straws. Let's count by 10s to make sure we have 100." After counting, say, "These 10 bundles of 10 (the same as 1 bundle of 100), represent the 100 shoes that little centipede wants to give away."

- Say, "Next we will add his 42 socks to the 100 shoes." Ask volunteers to help you show the number 42 with half-straws on the large place-value mat. When all of the straws have been placed, ask "How many bundles of 100 do we have? How many tens? How many ones?"

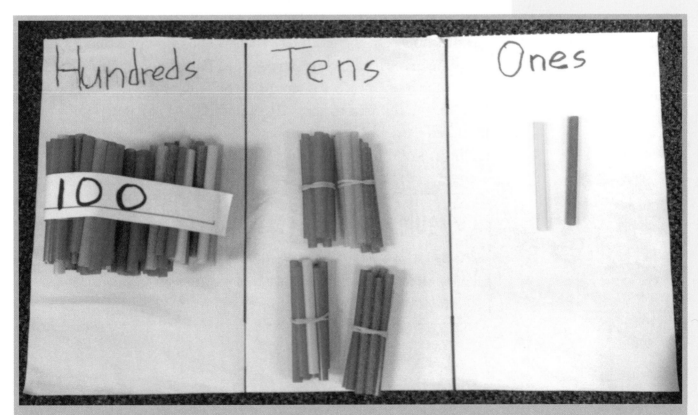

A picture book about a confused centipede is a fun opportunity to practice counting to a number in the hundreds.

- Finally, distribute individual place-value mats that can be used as recording sheets. Have students represent the number 142. Ask students to write the 1 hundred in red, the 4 tens in blue, and the 2 ones in green on their place-value mats. Re-count each place-value amount to show that the red 1 represents 100, the blue 4 represents 4 tens or 40, and the green 2 represents 2 ones.

- Say, "Now draw 1 bundle of 100 in red in the hundreds place; 4 bundles of 10 in blue in the tens place; 2 little straws in green in the ones place. Make sure each amount is in the correct place-value column." This takes the students' thinking from concrete to pictorial to abstract.

Extension: Use straws and/or bean sticks with similar problems, reinforcing the power of place value and of thinking in terms of 10s.

Whole Group

2.NBT.A.1a

Pennies to Dimes

Help students review and remember place value as they build up to three-digit numbers. This whole-year activity uses our monetary system, which is rooted in base 10. Add, or have a student add, a penny to a clear plastic sandwich bag each day, starting on the first day of school. On the tenth day, trade 10 pennies for a dime. Place the dime in a separate clear sandwich bag next to the pennies bag. Count the money each day, counting by tens, and then by ones. On Day 45, the children count, "10, 20, 30, 40, 41, 42, 43, 44, 45." On Hundred Day, empty the tens bag of dimes, and start a third bag containing a $1.00 bill.

> ✔ **QUICK TIP**
>
> *Because a penny is physically larger than a dime, many children are confused about trading 10 pennies for 1 dime. Make sure to show several other demonstrations of 10 ones becoming 1 ten, and of 10 tens becoming 1 hundred.*

Bag It!

Distribute resealable plastic bags and ask children to work in teams to fill each bag with 100 items. We like to use inexpensive cereal rings, Unifix cubes, centimeter cubes, bingo chips, or pennies. Anything small will work. Don't fill the bags yourself or have a volunteer do it. Your students need to do this so that they understand that you are working with sets of 100. You can use these bags to represent hundreds as kids count to 1,000: 100, 200, 300, and on to 1,000.

Show the class 1 filled bag and say, "This is 1 set of one hundred. Let's count it: 100." Next, hold up 2 filled bags and say, "This is 2 sets of one hundred. Let's count this: 100, 200." Hold up 3 filled bags and ask, "How many are there in all 3 of these bags?" Continue in this way, counting each new combination of bags until your children are comfortable with this model. Then put the bags down and ask the children to show you 700 pieces. Let a child volunteer show you 7 bags. Repeat this activity over a few days and watch your students build confidence and understanding.

*Whole Group,
Small Groups*

2.NBT.A.1b
Understand that the three digits of a three-digit number represent amounts of hundreds, tens, and ones; e.g., 706 equals 7 hundreds, 0 tens, and 6 ones. Understand the following as a special case: The numbers 100, 200, 300, 400, 500, 600, 700, 800, 900 refer to one, two, three, four, five, six, seven, eight, or nine hundreds (and 0 tens and 0 ones).

Counting to 700 by hundreds is easy using 7 bags of 100 pieces each.

✓ **QUICK TIP**

Keep the filled bags—you'll use them again for the activity Bagged Numbers on page 95.

Whole Group

2.NBT.A.2 Count
within 1000; skip-count
by 5s, 10s, and 100s.

How Much Is a Thousand?

 How Much Is a Million? by David M. Schwartz

Books like *How Much Is a Million?* get kids thinking about large numbers. Read the part about how long it would take to count to 1 million. Then introduce this activity by saying, "Can you count to 100 in 1 minute?" (Set the timer and have pairs of children attempt this.) Then hand out hundred charts and say, "We are going to use hundred charts to represent 100. Each of you has a hundred chart. How many hundred charts do we need to make 1,000?" Allow students time to think about this, then ask, "How long would it take us to count to 1,000 if it takes 1 minute to count 1 hundred chart?" By this time, your creative problem solvers will have started thinking up efficient ways to figure this out. Give them time to think this through—it's important for them to practice perseverance. Continue only after several children have given answers.

Continue by saying, "Use the hundred chart as we look at patterns for counting by 5s. What changes do you see? What is the pattern? Start at any 5 or 10 on the chart and count by 5s. What do you notice?" Allow time for children to discover the patterns themselves,

1–100 Chart

1	2	3	4	5	6	7	8	9	10
11	12	13	14	15	16	17	18	19	20
21	22	23	24	25	26	27	28	29	30
31	32	33	34	35	36	37	38	39	40
41	42	43	44	45	46	47	48	49	50
51	52	53	54	55	56	57	58	59	60
61	62	63	64	65	66	67	68	69	70
71	72	73	74	75	76	77	78	79	80
81	82	83	84	85	86	87	88	89	90
91	92	93	94	95	96	97	98	99	100

101–200 Chart

101	102	103	104	105	106	107	108	109	110
111	112	113	114	115	116	117	118	119	120
121	122	123	124	125	126	127	128	129	130
131	132	133	134	135	136	137	138	139	140
141	142	143	144	145	146	147	148	149	150
151	152	153	154	155	156	157	158	159	160
161	162	163	164	165	166	167	168	169	170
171	172	173	174	175	176	177	178	179	180
181	182	183	184	185	186	187	188	189	190
191	192	193	194	195	196	197	198	199	200

Have students use blank grid paper to create two hundred charts—one starting at 1, and another starting at 101. Let them use crayon or marker to color-code the ones in green, the tens in blue, and the hundreds in red. Use these colors consistently for these place values, and students will see the patterns more easily.

and be sure to praise those who are willing to describe what they discover in front of the class.

Keep using hundred charts to count by 10s and 100s. Continue to look for patterns and notice changes in place value. When children are comfortable with the first two charts, add a third chart so you can continue to 300. These are key anchor charts that deserve a place on your wall.

Extension: Show children how to count by 5s starting at a number other than 5 or 10. Start at 4 and count 9, 14, 19, 24, and so forth. Have them highlight these numbers in yellow and describe the pattern they see. Once they grasp counting by 5s starting at 4, try starting at 1, 2, or 3.

Map Quests

Whole Group

2.NBT.A.3 Read and write numbers to 1000 using base-ten numerals, number names, and expanded form.

A fun way to get students thinking about numbers in their world is to talk about distances in their state. A little time spent with an online map program will give you a wealth of numerical information about your part of the country. The sky is the limit!

Find answers to questions like these about your own state, and then use the numbers to practice reading and writing numbers to 1,000.

- How many miles is it from your school to your state capital?

- How many miles is it from your school to the largest city in your state?

- What is the length and width of your state?

Here are some examples from our home states of Tennessee and Florida:

- Tennessee is 440 miles across. Can you write this distance using number words? (four hundred forty; never say four hundred *and* forty)

- Driving from Nashville to Chattanooga on Interstate 24 is a distance of 133 miles. Let's write this number in words and in expanded form.

Finding distances using a map of your state generates plenty of opportunity to use large numbers. Live in a small state? Use a map of your region.

- The distance from Pensacola to Coral Springs is 642 miles. Write this number in expanded form and word form.

- Key West is 668 miles from the state capital, Tallahassee. It is one of the cities in Florida farthest from the capital.

*Small Groups,
Pairs, Individuals*

2.NBT.A.3

Food for Thought

Nutrition labels on boxes make a perfect place to find and write about numbers. You can use this as a homework activity or have students bring in packages and work in small groups.

Here's one example for how to use nutrition numbers. Say, "I found some corn chips in my pantry. If I ate one serving of these for 7 days in a row, how many calories would I be eating total?" Show how to solve the problem, then continue with how to write the answer. "I would be eating 980 calories. Can you write 980 in standard form, expanded form, and word form?"

Have the children find the answer to the problem using their own packages. Then have them write the answer in standard base-10 numerals, in expanded form, and in words. Make a display of the children's work, like the example shown on page 89. This is real-world math! Encourage students to look for number facts from 1 to 1,000 on food packages at home, too.

Save the food packages and the numbers you've gathered from them for Which Package Holds More? on page 90.

 QUICK TIP

You can create or purchase number word cards that allow a student to compose each number name quickly. Write the number words on strips of card stock and allow students to arrange the cards to "write" number words for practice, without having to write them by hand each time.

| one hundred | eighty | three |

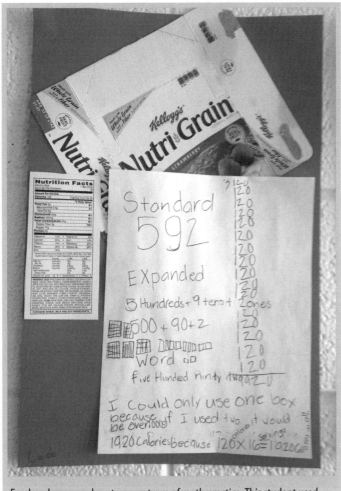

Food packages can be a treasure trove of math practice. This student used the nutrition facts to find the total calories in the package using both repeated addition and multiplication. Then he wrote the answer in standard form and expanded form, and as pictures of base-ten blocks.

Comparison Games

Kids play this game with one friend. Each child rolls 3 dice and then arranges the dots or numerals in the hundreds, tens, and ones places to form the largest number possible. The child then writes his number. His partner takes a turn, and then they compare their numbers using >, <, and =. Playing cards (minus the face cards) or 0 to 9 number cards also work well for this. Each child draws 3 cards from the deck and organizes them to form the largest possible number. The two children then write and compare their two numbers.

Pairs

2.NBT.A.4 Compare two three-digit numbers based on meanings of the hundreds, tens, and ones digits, using >, =, and < symbols to record the results of comparisons.

Which Package Holds More?

Gather the pantry items from Food for Thought on page 88 and draw >, =, and < symbols on some index cards. Order the foods from the least number of grams of food in the package to the greatest. Place the index cards with the < symbols between the items. Discuss the results. Next, invite student volunteers to order the items from the greatest to the least number of grams and place the > signs correctly. As you discuss the process, have children describe which numeral in which place value they look at first to decide which number is greater.

When students are finished comparing the weight of the boxes, ask, "How many boxes of each food would you need to buy to get as close as you can to 1,000 grams, but not buy more than 1,000 grams? Which food will you have the most packages of? Which food will you have the least packages of?" Encourage students to describe their thinking in answering these questions.

Extension: Place the materials at a center for individuals or pairs. Have students compare the packages by calories per serving. Point out that the total number of servings in a package is also listed. Ask them, "How many calories are in the whole package?"

To order the packages correctly, compare the number of grams in the packages. Lots of three-digit numbers!

Do any packages have equal weights? Stack them in the lineup!

Another way to show packages with the same weight is to place an
= sign between them.

GRADE ②

Cluster 2.NBT.B Use place value understanding and properties of operations to add and
subtract.

Whole Group

2.NBT.B.5 Fluently add
and subtract within 100
using strategies based on
place value, properties of
operations, and/or the
relationship between
addition and subtraction.

Adding Branches

This method, from Singapore, is a precursor for mental math that
relies solely on place value. It works like a charm. Once your students
have a handle on place value, they can easily add two-digit numbers
in their heads, which makes them feel brilliant! The girl in the photo
on page 92 is displaying how she solved a two-digit addition problem
using place value. You can lead your students through the strategy,
asking lots of questions. Here's an example:

- Say something like, "Let's say you want to add these two numbers:
  54 + 23." (Write this expression horizontally on a board.
  Encourage children to write it for themselves.)

- Next say, "If you break the numbers into their place values, what
  do you get? That's right: 54 becomes 50 and 4. The number 23
  becomes 20 and 3. Let's show what that looks like." (On the board,
  use expanded notation for each number, as the girl in the photo
  has.)

- Lead students through the rest of the process. Ask, "What happens
  when we add the tens together? That's right: we get 50 + 20, or 70;
  50 + 20 = 70." (Add this equation to your example.)

- Ask, "And what happens when we add the ones together? Yes, we get 4 + 3, or 7; 4 + 3 = 7."

- Ask, "Now how do we get the final answer? That's right: Put the 70 and the 7 together. What do we get? Yes, 77! You're such smart mathematicians. With some more practice, you can probably do these in your heads!"

UNDERSTANDING ADDITION

There are many ways to add 54 + 23. Many of us adults were taught only one way: line up the numbers vertically; add the numbers on the right, 4 + 3; write down the 7. Move to the left: 5 + 2 = 7; write down the 7; the answer is 77. While the answer is correct, doing it this way does not require or reinforce true understanding of place value—we are not adding 5 and 2; rather we are adding 5 tens and 2 tens, which is 7 tens, 70.

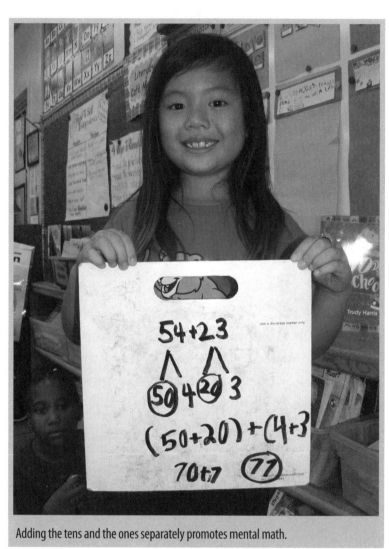

Adding the tens and the ones separately promotes mental math.

C P A
Whole Group

2.NBT.B.5

Subtracting Branches

When your children have mastered Singapore-style addition, try the same method for subtraction. How does it work? Simple! Just make sure to start with simple examples like 76 – 35, which do not require regrouping.

As with addition, subtraction starts with pulling the numbers apart using place value. Write 76 – 35 horizontally on the board, leaving room to write more beneath the expression.

- Say, "Let's break apart these two numbers. How many tens and how many ones are in 76? 76 is 7 tens and 6 ones. Let's branch them out below 76." (Write 70, circle it, and write 6 next to it.) Say, "Now let's do the same for 35; 35 is 3 tens and 5 ones." (Write 30 and 5 below 35, circling 30.)

- Continue with, "Now let's think about how to subtract the tens. What is 7 – 3? 7 – 3 is 4, so 7 tens minus 3 tens is 4 tens. Another way to say this is, 70 – 30 = 40." (Write this information on the board, matching what's done in the photo.)

- "Now it's time for the ones. How much is 6 – 5? 6 – 5 is 1."

- Talk students through this last part slowly. "So now we've subtracted the tens, and we've subtracted the ones. That's all there is to subtract. But we still need to do one other thing to get the difference—we need to *add* the two differences together." (Show this on the board: 40 + 1 = 41.) Say, "Our answer is 41."

Expanding numbers into their place values works for subtraction too; be sure to start with problems where regrouping is not needed.

 QUICK TIP

If any child is confused about why you would add at the end of a subtraction problem, bring out the bean sticks or other manipulatives and demonstrate what is happening until he understands. Encourage volunteers to explain it to their classmates, using manipulatives.

Three Times the Fun

Whole Group

Making a ten is a powerful strategy for adding two-digit numbers. We like to scaffold this strategy by starting out with numbers that easily make a ten, like these: 34 + 23 + 77 + 16 = ?

Have some base-10 blocks ready when you start discussing these numbers: hundred flats, ten rods, and one units.

- Show students the four numbers (34, 23, 77, 16). Say, "Let's check out the four numbers and see if there are any compatible numbers in either the tens place or the ones place. What do you see?" (Pause for deep thinking.)

2.NBT.B.6 Add up to four two-digit numbers using strategies based on place value and properties of operations.

✓ **QUICK TIP**

Demonstrate this important concept slowly to the children—do not rush this. Do not let children who catch on quickly rush the rest of the class, either. Give it time, so that students discover what it means to make a ten on their own. Give them enough practice so that it truly sinks in.

- Say, "Yes, the 3 in the tens place of 34 and the 7 in the tens place of 77 make a 10 when you add them together." (Show adding the tens first for 34 and 77. Represent the sum with rods from base-10 blocks: 3 tens + 7 tens = 10 tens or 100.)

- Show the 100 flat on a place-value mat. Say, "We still have 2 tens + 1 ten = 3 tens or 30." (Show the 3 tens with rods in the tens place.)

- Next, ask students to look at the ones place. "Are there any numbers in the ones place that are compatible to make a 10? Let's look: We have 3 ones + 7 ones = 10 ones or 1 ten." (Place 1 ten in the tens place with the other 3 tens.)

- "Lastly, we add the ones: 4 ones + 6 ones = 10 ones or 1 ten." (Place the last ten in the tens place with the other 4 tens.) "This gives us 5 tens for 50. Adding the hundred gives us a total of 150."

Give students lots of practice doing this over many days. Making a ten is a strategy that works for every place value, from the ones to the millions and beyond!

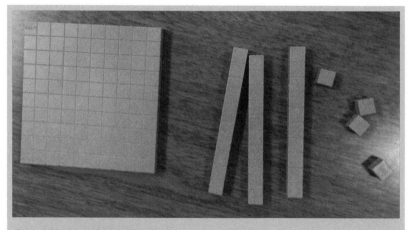

Base-10 blocks reinforce adding hundreds, tens, and ones. Large squares, also called *flats*, have 100 small squares. Ten small squares stuck together are called *rods* or *longs*. *Units* or *ones* are single small squares.

Bagged Numbers

You will need the bags of 100 small items from Bag It! (page 85), 10 small cups, each with 10 of the same item, and 10 more loose items. If the bags of items are not available, you can use sets of base-10 hundred blocks.

Begin simply by saying and modeling 200 + 700 = 900 using the class-made bags of 100 items. Then, write out more problems that add whole multiples of 100, and choose students to show the class how to use the models to find an answer for each problem. Once your students understand adding the sets of 100, crank it up a notch and say, "Watch this: 200 (2 bags of 100) 30 (3 cups of 10 items) plus 400 (4 bags of 100) equals 630." Write out the number sentence 230 + 400 = 630.

Give more problems like this, and then when children are comfortable adding tens and hundreds, change the numbers in the ones place to numbers other than 0, such as 236 + 423. You will be pleased at how deep your students' understanding becomes when they work slowly with these powerful models.

Whole Group

2.NBT.B.7 Add and subtract within 1000, using concrete models or drawings and strategies based on place value, properties of operations, and/or the relationship between addition and subtraction; relate the strategy to a written method. Understand that in adding or subtracting three-digit numbers, one adds or subtracts hundreds and hundreds, tens and tens, ones and ones; and sometimes it is necessary to compose or decompose tens or hundreds.

Decompose and Compensate

When you are adding and subtracting within 1,000 as a class, reinforce a deep conceptual understanding of place value. You want to be sure that your students can fluently compose and decompose numbers. For example, when your students see a problem like 900 – 49 = ?, seize the opportunity to use the benchmark of 50. Say, "Hey, 49 is only 1 less than 50. It's easy to take 50 away from 100. 900 – 50 = 850, right? But we weren't really subtracting 50. We were subtracting 49. Since 50 is 1 more than 49, we'll add 1 to our answer. So the answer is 851."

Problems like this also provide an opportunity to demonstrate compensation used while subtracting: take 1 from 900 to get 899, then take 1 from 49 to get 48. 899 – 48 = 851. This demonstrates a different approach that leads to the same correct answer.

Whole Group, Pairs

2.NBT.B.7

Variation: We love to use base-10 blocks on a base-10 mat with this type of problem. Give each pair of students 9 hundreds (a total of 900 units). At first, explore the numbers without using paper and pencil. Ask, "How can we take away 49?" Can they decompose one of the hundreds (flats) into 10 tens (rods)? Can they then decompose one of the tens (rods) into 10 ones (units) to allow them to take away 4 tens and 9 ones?

C P A
Small Groups

2.NBT.B.8 Mentally add 10 or 100 to a given number 100–900, and mentally subtract 10 or 100 from a given number 100–900.

Row, Row, Row by Ten

Hundred charts are the perfect game board for practicing –10 and +10. For each small group, you need a blank die (cube) and a hundred chart; each child also needs a game token. Write +10 on 3 sides of each die and –10 on the other 3 sides.

Introduce this game to the whole group before having children play in small groups of 2 to 4. Each child places a token on any one-digit number in the top row (1 to 9) of his hundred chart. The goal is to race to the last row (+90) from the starting place. The children take turns rolling the die. If a player rolls +10, then he moves

Using the hundred chart as a game board is a fun way to practice addition and subtraction facts.

his token to the number that is 10 more. If he rolls –10, then he moves back 10. If a token is in that top row, the player cannot move back 10, so he misses a turn. The winner is the first one to reach the last row of the chart.

Variation: This game can be played the same way for subtraction— just begin on the last row (90 to 100) instead of the first. The objective is to reach the top row.

Row Past a Hundred

Small Groups

2.NBT.B.8

When children have mastered Row, Row, Row by Ten above, they are ready for the place-value race to 1,000.

For this game, each child in each group of 2 to 4 needs her own place-value mat with ones, tens, hundreds, and thousands. Each group needs one die with +10 on two sides, –10 on one side, +100 on two sides, and –100 on one side. Children use base-10 blocks (flats and rods only) to show each roll. The first to reach 10 hundreds or 1 thousand wins.

The number represented on the mat changes with each roll of the special-sided die.

SEE WHAT THEY KNOW

Here's a problem you can use to uncover your students' thinking processes. Choose the format that works best for your students: reading the question aloud to the class or to small groups, or handing out a printed version for students to solve independently (see the copymaster on page 170). Provide some base-10 blocks so you can observe how students are solving the problem.

"Jennifer and Doris are playing Row Past a Hundred using base-10 blocks. Doris rolls +100 three times and −100 once. Jennifer rolls +100 two times, +10 nine times, and −100 once. Doris claims that she has the higher number. Jennifer disagrees; she thinks she has the higher number. Who is correct? Can you show who is correct using base-10 blocks?"

2.NBT.B.9 Explain why addition and subtraction strategies work, using place value and the properties of operations.

Show How You Compute!

Here's an activity you can do one-on-one or with small groups of students. Observing how students approach this problem will give you a clear understanding of what your students know, what level of thinking they are using (concrete, pictorial, or abstract), and where you need to focus your instruction.

Have these tools available: place-value blocks, bean sticks, Unifix cubes, straws in bundles of tens and in singles, 10-frames, and, if available, a 100-bead rekenrek like the one shown in the photo.

Write 43 + 27 for your students and then say, "Show me 43 + 27 using tools that you choose from the tools on this table." After a child shows you one way, ask, "Is there another way to show this?" If there is a second way, ask, "Can you use paper and pencil to tell me your thinking while you solved this equation?"

Listen for place-value language. Does the child know without thinking that 3 and 7 make a ten and they need to regroup? If the child can show you more than one way, pat yourself on the back! Piaget told us that children who use multiple strategies truly understand the concept.

Provide a variety of tools for students to use to add two-digit numbers, including a 100-bead rekenrek if you have one.

Measurement and Data

Length, volume, weight, and time are all abstract concepts, so it's important to make them as concrete as possible. Children need to hear what to do, ponder what it means, and answer questions that compare measurements. Who has a foot that's shorter than yours? Who has the shortest foot? Which object is lighter? Which object is heavier?

Make sure students see how measurement connects to their world. Start by brainstorming with your class. What would food taste like if cooks didn't measure ingredients? What would happen if a carpenter didn't measure lumber before building a house. Yikes! Measuring is very important!

Units of measure present challenges for primary grade children, who are not yet familiar with them. Can you weigh a box to determine how wide it is? Can you find out how much water is in a cup by using a ruler? "Fuzzy math" comments don't help. Mom might say, "I'll read to you in *just a minute,* after I call the neighbor, bathe your baby brother, and put the dishes away." Students must learn to recognize when a measurement is used as a figure of speech, and when it is meant to be precise.

Data may sound scientific—and it is— but the word simply refers to measurements your students have made. The more measurements your students make for a particular value, the more helpful it is to use charts or graphs to make sense of them. Data doesn't have to be dull—it can be about animals, sales from a lemonade stand, or any kid-friendly subject. When we make the learning engaging and interesting, our students will remember the lessons. That's what these activities are all about.

Go beyond workbook pages! Have your students make real measurements in the real world.

**Whole Group,
Small Groups, Pairs**

K.MD.A.1 Describe measurable attributes of objects, such as length or weight. Describe several measurable attributes of a single object.

GRADE K

Cluster K.MD.A Describe and compare measurable attributes.

How Long Is It?

Before young children understand or use units of measure, it's important for them to understand what it is they are measuring. What is length? What is width? Here are some ways to give your students lots of practice "measuring" the dimensions of an object.

Hold up a book and say, "I can measure the length of this book cover. Length is how long something is." Then demonstrate some ways to show the book's length. Cut string that equals the length of the book cover; lay paper clips along the length of the book; or lay the book on paper, and then trace a line on the paper showing the length of its cover. Remember, you are not talking about units of measure yet—only about the dimension being measured.

Introduce another way to talk about the book's size. Say, "How else can we measure this book? We measured the book cover's length. We can also measure the cover's width. Width is how wide, or how far across, something is." Use the same items that you used before— string, paper clips, and so forth—to show how you are measuring a different dimension of the same book cover.

Next, pose this question to the class: "What other things can we measure for length and width?" After they've made some suggestions, ask each child to measure whatever it is that he's chosen. He can draw a line that shows how long his foot is, another line that shows how long his finger is, and other lines that show the length of whatever other items he chooses to measure. Let your class cut twine, string, or yarn to show the lengths and widths of the items they've selected.

All About Us

Call two children up to the front of the group. Ask, "Who is taller? How do you know?" and "Who is shorter? How do you know?" As appropriate, compare other attributes, such as "Who has longer (or shorter) arms/legs/fingers/feet/hair?" Kids love conversations that center on them, so you will get lots and lots of play with this. Continue to call up kids in pairs so that your class has many opportunities to use comparative language.

C P A
Whole Group

K.MD.A.2 Directly compare two objects with a measurable attribute in common, to see which object has "more of"/"less of" the attribute, and describe the difference. *For example, directly compare the heights of two children and describe one child as taller/shorter.*

Best Bug Parade

 The Best Bug Parade by Stuart J. Murphy

This delightful book is all about comparing the sizes of colorful bugs. Read the book aloud as a class, discussing the statements the bugs make about how big and small they are. The charming illustrations and simple text will make this a best-loved book at your reading center. Add simple finger puppets for more fun!

C P A
*Whole Group,
Individuals*

K.MD.A.2

Decorate the fingers of inexpensive garden gloves with pom-poms and googly eyes to make bugs that are fun to use when acting out the comparisons in the book.

Pairs, Individuals

K.MD.A.2

Veggie-Table

Gather a variety of sturdy, fresh vegetables that are longer than they are wide, such as carrots and celery sticks. Place the veggies at a math center table. Use tape to divide the table into a simple two-part chart, and then label one side *Longer* and the other side *Shorter*. Center partners take 2 ears of corn, compare their lengths, and then place one in the *Longer* column and one in the *Shorter* column. Or, they take 2 different kinds of vegetables and make the same comparison. Partners continue until all veggies have been compared. The next set of partners comes to the center and checks their classmates' labels.

Expect dialogue like, "This corn is longer than that corn," and "That carrot is shorter than that celery." Eavesdrop and praise that language when you hear it! For children who struggle to get started, it helps for an adult to hand the child two vegetables at a time. This eliminates the time they take for decision making, if there are too many veggies to select from.

Variation: Use flowers from a bouquet that has lasted as long as a bouquet can last, strips of paper, used pencils or crayons, pieces of rope, or any other "long" objects.

Extension: Have children who need more of a challenge line up the veggies in order of length. Since they are comparing more than two objects, they'll need to go beyond comparative language (shorter, longer) and use superlative language (shortest, longest).

How Many Shoes Are You?

Pairs

K.MD.A.2

Ask each child to remove one shoe. (This is already a hit—they love to take off their shoes!) Say, "You're going to measure a friend, and a friend is going to measure you. We're going to find out how many shoes tall you are." Demonstrate with one child lying on the floor. Place one of that child's shoes at the child's heels. Put your finger at the top of the shoe, and then move the shoe so it's immediately above your finger. Continue until you've measured the full length of the child. Say, "You are 5 shoes tall (or however many shoes you've measured, rounded off to the nearest shoe)." Have your students pair off and repeat the process. Then compare results and discuss: "Do most children have the same number of shoes for their height? Is it typical for 5 shoes to equal 1 kindergartner in this class?"

If length vs. height comes up, make sure students understand that even though they are lying on the floor, it is their height being measured and not their length—or, that their length when they are lying down is the same as their height when they are standing up.

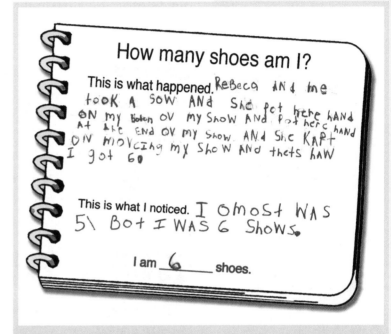

Math Journal: Have children record how they measured their height in shoes, using words or pictures.

Extension: Challenge your sharpest kids to measure a friend's height in Unifix cubes. Children need to be able to count beyond 30 to do this.

 SEE WHAT THEY KNOW

Are your students getting the hang of measurement? Observe them in small groups or individually. Provide string, yarn, scissors, Unifix cubes, and whatever other measuring materials your students have used. Set out a variety of objects that they can measure.

Ask, "What would you like to show me that you can measure? Can you tell me what you are thinking as you measure it?"

C P A
Pairs, Individuals

K.MD.A.2

Weigh Everything You Can

Children must have experiences weighing objects in order to understand weight. Looking at pictures in a book cannot begin to help a child understand that a rock weighs more than a feather or a pair of scissors. She needs to hold items in her hands and compare their weights. She needs to pour, fill, and refill containers, comparing the weights of containers of different sizes filled with different materials. She needs to balance items on a scale. *That's* how a child internalizes these concepts. So, place a balance scale at the Veggie-Table (page 102) that your children can use to compare weight. Let children compare which veggies are heavier and which are lighter. Encourage conversation such as, "The celery stick is lighter than the ear of corn."

Extension: Have students compare fruit, books, classroom supplies, or math manipulatives. Remember that your little charges need repeated practice with a variety of items in order to internalize the concept and extend it to their experiences with the world.

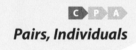

C P A
Pairs, Individuals

K.MD.A.2

How Much Will It Hold?

Volume refers to the amount of space something takes up. *Capacity* is the space available in a container. Set up a center where your charges can spend lots of time pouring rice, beans, or water from one container into another. It is important that the containers vary in both height and width, as well as the size of their openings. Children are often surprised when they discover that the short, wide container holds more than the tall, thin container. Ask students to use language to compare the containers, such as, "This bowl holds more rice than this pitcher" or "The cup holds fewer beans than the jar."

Young children may or may not need to understand the difference between the terms *volume* and *capacity*, but they do need to understand and compare these attributes!

 **QUICK TIP**

There is a simple reason why the short, wide container holds more than the tall, thin container. The capacity of a cylinder is affected much more by diameter than by height.

GRADE **K**

Cluster K.MD.B Classify objects and count the number of objects in each category.

The activities for this cluster are engaging, kid-tested, teacher-approved ways to sort with your students. Once the sorting is complete for any activity, ask children to look at each group and estimate which group has more. After children have given their estimates, count each set and compare the numbers. Snag this opportunity to model math talk about the numbers being greater than, less than, or equal to other numbers.

This is also a great time to show your students the one-to-one way to compare the numbers. For instance, if there are more red lids than blue lids, make a nice straight row of all the red lids. Next to that, make a row of all the blue lids, so that a blue lid is across from a red lid. It will be easy to see that there are more red lids since the line of red lids continues beyond the line of blue lids. You can see an example of red and blue bears compared this way on page 27.

Where Does This Belong?

Ask each child to give you one shoe. (All will laugh. Some will dramatically cover their noses and gag. Kids are real actors!) Pile the shoes by your side. Seat single-shoed children in a circle around you. Start sorting shoes into 2 separate sets—Velcro and non-Velcro—but do not tell the children *how* you are sorting the shoes (aka the sorting rule).

Once you have placed 3 or 4 shoes in each set, ask the students if they can figure out how you sorted the shoes. If they are not able to identify the rule, continue sorting until a child can explain the rule. Once someone has figured out the rule, discuss the attributes of the finished sets. Ask, "Which set has more shoes? Which has fewer shoes? What is the difference in the number of shoes in these sets? How many Velcro shoes are there? How many non-Velcro shoes are there?"

Use the same shoes to sort again. This time, sort by "white soles" and "another color of sole." Again, do not tell the class your rule; let them figure it out. Continue with the same sort of questions you used for the Velcro sort. Ask, "Can any of you smart mathematicians come up with another sorting rule?"

✔ **QUICK TIP**

Share the activities for Cluster K.MD.B with your fellow primary teachers in first and second grade. Kids love to sort, and sorting should not end in kindergarten.

Whole Group

K.MD.B.3 Classify objects into given categories; count the numbers of objects in each category and sort the categories by count.

Extension: A slightly more challenging sort deals with numbers, for example: "All buttons with 2 holes go over here; all buttons with more than 2 holes go over here." Or, "If you have 4 members in your family, stand here; if you have fewer than 4 or more than 4 members in your family, stand over here."

C P A

Whole Group

K.MD.B.3

Hat Day

 Caps for Sale by Esphyr Slobodkina

 Hats Hats Hats by Ann Morris

Choose a day to ask kids to come to school wearing their favorite hats. Begin the day by reading aloud either the storybook *Caps for Sale* or the nonfiction book *Hats Hats Hats.* After that, sort kids by the hats they are wearing and then count the number of hats in each category. Think of the possibilities: with brims and without brims; colors; straw vs. cloth vs. knit vs. another material; hats for certain sports teams; hats printed with pictures, words, or both; printing in block letters, cursive, or neither; with buttons or without buttons.

Remember to talk about the groups after each sort. For example, "There are 11 kids in the group of hats with the names of sports teams and 7 kids in the group of hats without the name of a sports team. Eleven is more than 7. Seven is less than 11. Which group is larger? Which is smaller?"

You could spend all day sorting kids by the hats they are wearing. Choose categories, and then count the number of hats in each category. Choose a different category and count again.

Flip Your Lids!

C P A

*Small Groups,
Pairs, Individuals*

K.MD.B.3

Lids are wonderful for sorting! They have countless sorting possibilities. Ask families to send in clean lids and caps from an assortment of bottles, such as shampoo, milk, jelly, margarine, salad dressing, peanut butter, orange juice, and anything else they have on hand. Place all the lids and caps in a container at a center. Children may sort lids and caps by color, by caps that have words and those that do not, with pictures and without pictures, small and large, metal and plastic, and so on. The kids will think of ways to sort the lids that you haven't even considered.

Kid Sorts

C P A

Whole Group

K.MD.B.3

The best manipulatives are the kids themselves! Kid Sorts are a great way to fill a few minutes at the end of the day with fun and practice. Your students will come up with great ideas for sorting themselves. To get them started, try any of these sorting rules:

- Shirts: Sort by collar and no collar, words and no words, pictures and no pictures, pockets and no pockets.

- Pants: Sort by jeans and not jeans, long and not long, pockets and no pockets.

- Hair: Sort by color, curly and not curly, ponytail and no ponytail and, of those with ponytails, hair scrunchies and no scrunchies.

- Accessories: backpacks and other kinds of bags, mittens and gloves, shoes and boots, jackets and vests.

SORT IT OUT!

After the children have watched and helped you sort a variety of items, it's time to turn things over to them. All too often, well-meaning teachers pass out the objects and say, "Okay, now sort these fabric swatches by designs and no designs." But that removes part of the math from your lesson.

Your job is to pass out the materials to be sorted. Their job is to decide the sorting rule and then sort. Let them sort, and then let them tell the class the sorting rule they came up with. Even better, let them write their rules in their math journals as a perfect closure to the lesson. On another day, do it again. Any lesson like this needs to be repeated many times to be sure students have really got the idea!

GRADE 1

Cluster 1.MD.A Measure lengths indirectly and by iterating length units.

1.MD.A.1 Order three objects by length; compare the lengths of two objects indirectly by using a third object.

Super Superlatives

Call three kids to the front of the class. Say, "I am looking at the heights of all three people. Hmm . . . I'm going to put Ryan here because he is the shortest." Move Ryan to the group's far right. "And Adam, you are the tallest, so you are going to stand here." Place Adam at the left. "Now, Leslie, you are shorter than Adam, but taller than Ryan, so you are going in the middle."

Continue this type of conversation with the children while comparing other objects. For example, cut three different lengths of rope, string, or yarn. Say, "When I measure something from the ground up, that is called height; but when I measure from one end to the other, that is called length. So, let's look at these three pieces of rope. Can someone line up these pieces of rope from shortest to longest?"

Once children understand the relative lengths of the pieces of rope, continue comparing other objects. "Let's look at the tables." Point out three tables in the classroom that have three different, easily observable lengths. For example, "Look at this table where four children work, my desk, and the table by my chair. Of these three, which table is longest and which is shortest?"

Take an in-school field trip to find three articles whose sizes you can compare, just by observing. For example, in the school office the front desk is longer than the side table, but not as long as the carpet runner. On the playground, the monkey bars are longer than the balance beam, and the balance beam is longer than the hopscotch game. Encourage the children to come up with sentences to compare these lengths, such as, "The hopscotch game is long; the balance beam is longer; and the monkey bars are longest," and "The balance beam is longer than the hopscotch game but shorter than the monkey bars."

Start comparing size by comparing three students: tall, taller, tallest.

Stuffed Animal Belt Size

Set out a variety of stuffed animals. (Now you really have their attention!) Select any three stuffed animals, and ask the kiddos, "If we were going to make belts for these three stuffed friends, which one would need the shortest belt? Which would need the longest belt? Let's find out."

Ask a child to wrap string or ribbon around the tummy of each animal and then cut the string where it meets. The length of each of the three strings equals its stuffed animal's girth, or the length of the belt that animal would need. Once all three strings are cut, ask students to line up the strings in order of shortest to longest and set each animal behind its string. After all three "belts" have been compared, ask students to make up sentences that use comparing words to describe the belts.

> ✔ **QUICK TIP**
>
> *You do not need to use the term <u>circumference</u> to describe the distance around the animal's tummy; however, some little Einstein in your class would love to use that word if you choose to introduce it. Other children will ignore a word with that many syllables and just continue measuring with string. Either response is fine!*

Math Journal: Students who are able to write may describe the different lengths of the stuffed friends' belts in their math journals.

Extension: This extension develops skills addressed in Standard 1.MD.A.2. Ask students to record the length of each belt in Unifix cubes or another nonstandard unit.

Kids will fall hook, line, and sinker for such a preposterous idea as measuring a stuffed animal for a belt.

Ladybugs & Others

 The Grouchy Ladybug by Eric Carle

A grouchy ladybug challenges animals of ever-increasing size in the classic book *The Grouchy Ladybug*. Both the animals and the type font get larger with each page turn. Read the book as a class, and then prepare students to use it at a center. Place the book on a table, and model for students some methods for comparing the lengths of the critters and the sizes of the fonts. Use string, Unifix cubes, centimeter cubes, paper-clip chains—whatever is handy. Tell children to measure each creature at its widest or tallest point. With the exception of the snake, which happens to be wrapped around a tree, the animals are fairly easy to measure. For the type fonts, have them measure the tallest letter available.

Extension: As a challenge, children may record the length of each animal in chart form, with the name of each animal in one column and its length or height in the next column.

*Whole Group,
Individuals*

1.MD.A.2 Express the length of an object as a whole number of length units, by laying multiple copies of a shorter object (the length unit) end to end; understand that the length measurement of an object is the number of same-size length units that span it with no gaps or overlaps. *Limit to contexts where the object being measured is spanned by a whole number of length units with no gaps or overlaps.*

Are All Crayons Equal?

Use a nonstandard unit with varying size to demonstrate the importance of using units that are all identical. Say, "If I measured the length of this table using crayons from the same brand-new box, it would work well, correct? Because all the crayons are the same length." Demonstrate this with help from a few mathematicians. Have them lay the crayons from a new box end-to-end along the edge of the table and count the total number of crayons. (Ignore any leftover table at the end; the students are measuring to the nearest whole unit.)

Next say, "But what if I pulled the crayons out of the class crayon box? I would have some very small crayons that have worked hard for us this year and some brand-new crayons that are much longer." Demonstrate this to the doubting crowd at your feet by using crayons in all sorts of lengths. Deliberately choose crayons that are "near the end of the road in crayon life" and some that are brand-new. Count the crayons together as a class. Then clear the crayons away and do it again using a different assortment from the used crayon box. Ask students what happens to the "length in crayons" of the table when you use crayons of different lengths.

Variation: A great center activity is to leave a variety of nonstandard units (for example, paper clips or Unifix cubes) that can be used to measure whatever their little hearts desire.

Cereal & Cracker Rulers

Pairs, Individuals

1.MD.A.2

Create nonstandard rulers using Mini-Wheats cereal, Cheez-It crackers or their generic equivalents. Cut poster board or foam-core board into 1 × 12-inch strips. Provide glue and cereal or crackers. (Remind children not to "eat the math"!) Give one strip to each child. Have the kids write their names on one side and then turn the strips over. Have each child glue 12 pieces in a row to each strip to create a "ruler" and let them dry overnight.

When the rulers are dry and ready, ask, "How many items can you find in the room that are exactly 1 Mini-Wheat long or 1 Cheez-It long?" "How many items are 2 Mini-Wheats long or 2 Cheez-Its long?" Continue asking through 12. The cool thing about Cheez-Its is that each cracker is about 1 inch long. So an item that is 4 Cheez-Its long is about 4 inches long! The same is true for many Mini-Wheat varieties.

Rulers with nonstandard units help to develop the concept of units of measure.

C P A

Pairs, Individuals

1.MD.A.2

Inchworms

 Inch by Inch by Leo Lionni

Read *Inch by Inch* with your class. Have children create their own inchworms by gluing tiny pom-poms to 1-inch squares of foam or paper and then gluing each square to the end of a craft stick. Students can measure items in the room using their own inchworms. These inchworms are also good for helping children put spaces between words when they're writing.

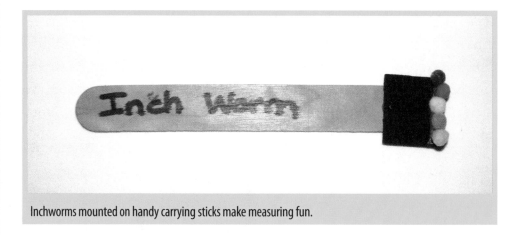

Inchworms mounted on handy carrying sticks make measuring fun.

GRADE ①

Cluster 1.MD.B Tell and write time.

Whole Group

1.MD.B.3 Tell and write time in hours and half-hours using analog and digital clocks.

Time Talk

Classic, colorful Judy Clocks are the perfect teaching aid for telling time on an analog (dial) clock. If you can get your hands on a small Judy Clock for every student, do it! Have each child move the hands of her clock to match the hands on your large clock. If you do not have access to Judy Clocks, handmade paper-plate clocks work just fine. Attach the hands with brass brads so the hands can be easily moved.

We practice with Judy Clocks by telling stories to our students—stories about them! They love doing this. Here's an example. Make up others based on your students' lives.

• "It was 9:00 A.M. on Saturday, and Zack was eating cereal." (Everyone moves the clock hands to 9:00.)

Judy Clocks are a time-tested tool for learning to read a dial clock.

Allow children to explore their little clocks when they first get their hands on them—otherwise, they will be playing with the clocks while you are trying to teach.

- "At 10:00 A.M., Zack got his hockey equipment together." (Everyone moves the clock hands to 10:00.)

- "By 11:00 A.M., Zack was in the car and ready to go!" (Everyone moves the clock hands to 11:00.)

You will have a captive audience, as every child wants to hear a simple story about himself. Tell time stories all year long, progressing from stories with times only on the hour to stories with times on the hour and on the half hour. By midyear, the children start to tell their own time stories, too.

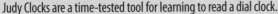

Read About Time

 The Very Hungry Caterpillar by Eric Carle

 The Grouchy Ladybug by Eric Carle

Read *The Very Hungry Caterpillar*. This story is a good way to review and discuss the idea of time, using a unit of time that can be observed in nature (days). Discussing the passage of days in this story lays the foundation for understanding hours, which are units of time created by people. After you read the story, discuss the time lapse from page to page and the total time lapse from the beginning of the story to the end.

C P A
Whole Group

1.MD.B.3

Next, read or reread *The Grouchy Ladybug*. If possible, have a classroom-sized Judy Clock nearby. As you read, move the hands on the Judy Clock to match the time as each new character enters the story. If your students have individual Judy Clocks or paper clocks, they should move the hands on their individual clocks at the same time. Discuss the passage of time from page to page and from the beginning of the book to the end.

Real-Life Time

As a teacher, you must constantly keep track of time—so use your clock-watching to teach time to your students! For example, say, "We have lunch in 15 minutes. The clock will look like this." (Draw a quick sketch on the board or move the hands on the class Judy Clock.) Or, "The assembly is at 10:30 A.M. That's 2 hours from now. Here is what the clock will look like." "I hope to meet with the Panther reading group in 10 minutes, at 9:00 A.M."

How often do you say this? "I'm giving you 5 minutes until cleanup." Now, this is a hard statement to stick to! But you must. If you say, "5 minutes until cleanup," be true to your word. If you let 5 minutes drift into 10 because the students are deeply into their work and you don't want to stop them, then you'll only confuse them about how long 5 minutes lasts, as well as what 5 elapsed minutes look like on an analog or digital clock.

Instead, at 5 minutes say, "I told you we'd clean up in 5 minutes. As I look around I can see that you are still working, so I'm going to give you 5 more minutes." That way, your little charges have enough time to finish, while still understanding 5 minutes.

The same thing goes for when you need to end earlier than expected. If you've told the students they have 10 minutes more and bedlam ensues after 3 minutes because they've all finished, then say, "I know I told you 10 minutes more, but I can see that you're all done. So even though it's only been 3 minutes, let's clean up. Good for you!"

Cluster 1.MD.C Represent and interpret data.

Graphing with Objects

1.MD.C.4 Organize, represent, and interpret data with up to three categories; ask and answer questions about the total number of data points, how many in each category, and how many more or less are in one category than in another.

With your kids, gather some data to graph. Fun questions like the ones listed below are one way to generate data. Or, ask students to bring in a certain kind of object and then sort them. However you gather your data, the point of this standard is to organize the data and then show it in such a way that it's easy to interpret.

Maybe each child has brought in the box from her favorite cereal. (This is fun to graph, even if the boxes take up lots of space!) Talk students through sorting the boxes and using them to create a life-size graph.

Say, "How shall we sort these boxes?" Pause. *Long* pause. If no one makes a suggestion, say, "I see we have sweetened cereal and unsweetened cereal. So maybe I could make a row of sweetened cereal. I'll line up all the boxes from sweetened cereal in a row." Move the sweetened-cereal boxes into a line.

Next say, "Now I'm going to take the unsweetened cereals and put *those* boxes in a row next to the first line. That way I can see without counting which kind of cereal I have more of. I need to be sure to put my first box in line with the first sweetened-cereal box. Then I have to make sure that each box in the unsweetened line is directly across from a box in the sweetened line, even if the boxes are all different sizes." Demonstrate how the boxes line up, one across from the other.

Say, "This is a graph of cereal boxes. The graph shows which kind of cereal we have more of. I can see that the line of sweetened cereal is much longer. There are 9 more boxes in the sweetened-cereal line

GOOD TOPICS FOR GRAPHING

- *What color are your eyes (or hair)?*
- *Are you the oldest, youngest, middle, or only child in your family?*
- *What color is the car you ride in most often?*
- *What color socks / shirt / pants are you wearing today?*
- *What is your favorite flavor of ice cream / cereal / fruit / cafeteria lunch / board game / holiday / restaurant / sports team / outdoor activity?*

than in the unsweetened-cereal line. I can tell because the sweetened-cereal line extends out 9 boxes beyond the unsweetened-cereal line."

When you're sure everyone is with you, ask "Can anyone think of another way to sort these boxes, one that would put our boxes in 3 categories (lines) instead of 2?" Allow some time for pondering. There are countless ways to sort these boxes and, given time, your kiddos will start to rattle off ways to sort that you haven't thought of, such as, "These cereals are made with wheat; these are made with oats; and these are made with bran." Or, "These are circles; these are square shapes; and these are mixed-up shapes." Let children sort out the boxes into the 3 (or more!) groups they've identified, forming a bar graph of the objects themselves.

All children do better when their understanding is grounded in the concrete. Building a graph using the actual objects is as concrete as you can get! Once students have experience with the concrete, bump things up a notch by representing data with pattern blocks or blocks from the block center. These materials are still concrete, of course, but because they're more abstract than boxes, they help to build student understanding.

 SEE WHAT THEY KNOW

Provide several sets of manipulatives that can be sorted in some way. Meet with your students one at a time, read the following task, and observe how they approach it. Can your student do this without prompting? Does the child see more than one way to sort? Does the child use precise language to describe the sorting rule?

"Here are several sets of things that we have sorted in class. Pick one of these sets and sort them. Tell me what you are thinking as you sort and what your sorting rule is. Then do something to show what you found out when you sorted them—like which category has more or fewer things in it."

Picture This!

Once your students have had lots of practice sorting, organizing, and graphing concrete materials, it is time to move on to picture graphs, also known as pictographs. Provide small paper shapes that represent the objects being graphed, for example triangles for pizza slices or circles for clock faces. It is critical that all of the paper shapes are congruent so that when the graph is assembled, no one shape stands out. Let each child decorate her shape to show her own personal data point, whether it is a favorite type of pizza or a bedtime hour. (Bedtime lets you practice 2 standards at once, since children also get practice showing clock time!)

When children have decorated their shapes, assemble the graphs. Label each graph with a title, a key, and labels for the horizontal and vertical axes. A pizza graph might have the following information:

- Title: Favorite Pizzas in Our Class

- Key: 1 pizza slice = 1 person's vote

- Horizontal axis labels: cheese, pepperoni, other

- Vertical axis label: number of votes

You can make pictographs around any class data set, not just favorite pizzas. This bulletin-board pictograph, titled "When Is Your Birthday?," uses gift bags to represent data points. The horizontal axis is labeled with months of the year; the vertical axis is labeled with the number of students whose birthdays fall in each month.

GRADE 2

Cluster 2.MD.A Measure and estimate lengths in standard units.

2.MD.A.1 Measure the length of an object by selecting and using appropriate tools such as rulers, yardsticks, meter sticks, and measuring tapes.

Make a Yard

 Inchworm and a Half by Elinor J. Pinczes

 How Big Is a Foot? by Rolf Myller

This engaging game is great for a math center. Provide a yardstick, three 1-foot rulers, 1 die, and a bowl of 12 objects that are each 1 inch long. Children play the game alone, or on the floor with a partner. A photo of two children playing a similar game, Make a Meter, appears on page 120. Partners take turns rolling the die and placing that number of 1-inch objects along the edge of one of the 1-foot rulers. When the objects total 12 inches (1 foot), the child places the 1-foot ruler on the yardstick, puts the objects back in the bowl, and starts on the next foot. The goal is to build 3 feet (1 yard). Students quickly see that it takes 12 inches to make 1 foot and 3 feet to equal 1 yard.

The books listed above make great companion reads for this center. *Inchworm and a Half* gets into fractions later in the book, which is beyond the scope of this standard.

Variation: Place two complete sets of rulers and objects at a center, and allow student pairs to play competitively.

2.MD.A.2 Measure the length of an object twice, using length units of different lengths for the two measurements; describe how the two measurements relate to the size of the unit chosen.

How Tall Is Your Flower?

Is this science or math? The answer is "YES!" Your children will draw three plants and measure their heights using two different units: inches and centimeters.

You will need some local plants (also called wildflowers or weeds), inch rulers, and metric rulers. You can collect the plants yourself to bring into the classroom, take your students outdoors to collect plants, or take your students outdoors with rulers to measure the plants without collecting them. Note: Be sure to check your state's guidelines on the use of natural materials in the classroom before conducting this activity. Also, scout the grounds ahead of time and avoid collecting in areas with poison ivy or other "don't-touch-me" plants.

Place children in groups of three to do the measurement activity. Each group works with one plant at a time. One child draws the plant on a sheet of paper. (The child may simply trace a line the height of the plant, rather than taking time to draw it.) A second child measures the height of the plant in inches, while the third measures it in centimeters. Have children record all measurements and the units.

When all groups have finished, lead a class discussion about the height of each plant. How tall is it in inches? How tall in centimeters? Is it the plant that's different or the unit of measurement?

Measuring the same object using two different units of measure helps to clarify the dimensions of inches and centimeters.

 QUICK TIP

Some plants spread along the ground instead of growing tall. If that's the case, have children measure the width of the plant rather than its height, and ask all groups to write down whether their measurement is height or width.

Make a Meter

Pairs

2.MD.A.3 Estimate lengths using units of inches, feet, centimeters, and meters.

This fun-filled activity bears repeating as your children build a solid understanding of the concept of centimeters and meters, which is the foundation for making estimates. A base-10 unit block is 1 centimeter square; the rods (or longs) are 10 centimeters long (1 decimeter) and 1 cm wide. You will need metersticks, base-10 blocks, and dice. We bag 10 rods/tens, 10 units/ones, and a die in a sandwich bag. We sometimes throw in a few extra units/ones per bag, since those seem to go missing more often than the other blocks.

Play this game in pairs. Place a meterstick on the floor. Two children sit on opposite sides of the meterstick. The first child rolls the die, places units on his side of the meterstick to represent the roll, and then announces how many centimeters total are shown. Then the

✓ QUICK TIP

So much of what you do in the primary grades lays a foundation for the later grades. Your students will draw on their deep understanding of centimeters and meters in the intermediate grades when they have to express 12 centimeters as 12/100 of a meter or 0.12 meter.

second child takes a turn. When the first child's turn comes around again, he adds unit blocks to the original row, and announces the new total. For example, for a first roll of 5, the student places 5 units along the meterstick starting at 0, and says "5 centimeters." If he rolls a 6 on his second turn, he doesn't have enough unit blocks to show the total. He has to swap 10 unit blocks for one rod, place it along the meterstick starting at zero, and then add 1 more unit to show 11 centimeters. (Another benefit is that this activity reinforces addition facts, and tens and ones!) The game continues until one child reaches 100 centimeters or 1 meter.

Second graders have a ball with this game. They very quickly begin to call the rod a decimeter stick. The blocks provide benchmarks for centimeters and decimeters, and the game develops their understanding that it takes 100 centimeters to make a meter.

These children are building meters *and* building understanding!

Estimating Length

Estimation becomes easy as units of measure become second nature—but that takes practice. Give your students practice estimating metric lengths. Cut five different colors of ribbon into five different lengths. For example, cut red ribbon 10 cm long, blue 20 cm, green 40 cm, yellow 50 cm, and orange 100 cm (1 m). Divide the class into five groups, or make two sets of ribbons and divide into ten groups.

Give each group one length of ribbon, but do not give out any rulers or metersticks. Ask each group to estimate the length of the ribbon in centimeters, and then write down the ribbon color and their agreed-upon estimate. Then have each group swap ribbons with another group. Repeat until all groups have made estimates for every color of ribbon.

Next, record all of the estimates for the length of each ribbon color on one class chart. Discuss the estimates. Ask students to share how they went about making their estimates. Then, bring out the rulers and metersticks and have student volunteers measure the length of each ribbon. Discuss the results. Which group came closest for each color? How close was the closest estimate? How does estimating and then measuring help you to make a better estimate next time?

Variations: Repeat this activity with string, a sheet of paper, the classroom flag, a pencil, or the width of a door. Use these same strategies for estimating length in inches, feet, and yards: any activity that lets students use what they have learned to make an estimate, and then check their estimates against a measuring tool.

Small Groups

2.MD.A.3

Actual Size

 Actual Size by Steve Jenkins

In the beautifully illustrated picture book *Actual Size,* Steve Jenkins provides a menagerie of animals to measure and compare. Some of the animals are truly giant, so take this activity outdoors or into the hallway. Place students into small groups of 2 to 4. Bring something to mark the starting points for measuring (we use orange cones from the gym), and for each group, yardsticks and inch rulers, as well as paper and pencils to collect and record data.

Small Groups

2.MD.A.4 Measure to determine how much longer one object is than another, expressing the length difference in terms of a standard length unit.

The giant squid is an impressive animal to start with. Its body and tentacles measure up to 59 feet long. Place the starting markers at one point, and start measuring! Some groups will use yardsticks and count by 3s to measure because they remember that 3 feet equals 1 yard from the Make a Yard activity on page 118. Others will use inch rulers. Either approach is fine. When all groups have finished measuring, place one marker at a location that all groups can agree on to indicate the end of the giant squid.

Parallel to the measurement for the giant squid, show the length of the next animal from Steve's book. The man-eating, saltwater crocodile is the largest reptile in the world. It grows to a length of 23 feet. Have groups measure this length starting at the same place as the giant squid, and mark the end. Wow, what a difference! Ask, "What do you think? How much longer is the giant squid compared with the saltwater crocodile?" Encourage students to share their estimates of the difference in length of the two creatures.

Extension: Challenge groups to calculate and record the difference in length between a giant squid and a saltwater crocodile. Gather the groups to discuss their findings. Would 2 crocodiles placed end-to-end be longer or shorter than 1 giant squid?

The book *Actual Size* has many amazing animal measurements that make for great classroom activities. Here, students measure out the actual size of a gorilla's arm span.

> ✓ **QUICK TIP**
>
> *We post measurements like the length of the giant squid where kids can see them. Later in the year, we might be reading a book that tells the height of a giant redwood tree. Having the squid measurement posted lets us go back and compare.*

GRADE 2

Cluster 2.MD.B Relate addition and subtraction to length.

Exploring Animal Sizes

 Actual Size by Steve Jenkins

Actual Size can be a source of many rich problems involving two-digit addition and subtraction of real-life length measurements. Here is one example to get you started.

Problem: "The giant walking stick insect is 22 inches long. The combined length of the giant walking stick and the giant Gippsland earthworm is 58 inches. How long is the giant Gippsland earthworm?" Explore this problem as a class, using a variety of methods to ensure students understand it at a deep level:

- Write an equation for the problem, using a symbol for the unknown length of the giant Gippsland earthworm: 22 + ? = 58.

- Represent the problem using concrete materials. For example: Lay 58 1-inch tiles or 58 1-inch crackers (such as Cheez-Its) end to end.

- Bridge to abstract representation of the problem using place-value cards and bean sticks (page 74) or place-value cards with unit blocks to show 5 tens and 8 ones.

- Ask, "What part of the equation 22 + ? = 58 do we know?" (The length of the giant walking stick and the total length of both critters together.) "What part of the equation do we want to find out?" (The length of the giant Gippsland earthworm.)

- Ask, "How can we use these materials to help solve the problem?" (Students may suggest taking 22 crackers from the row of 58, or 2 tens and 2 ones from the place-value mat.)

- Ask, "What number is left?" (36) "What does it stand for? Is it the length of the giant earthworm in inches? How do you know?" (If some students do not understand that the difference is the length of the earthworm, draw a quick picture showing the worm and the stick insect end to end, label each with its length, and write the number sentence 22 + 36 = 58 above them.)

C P A
Whole Group, Individuals

2.MD.B.5 Use addition and subtraction within 100 to solve word problems involving lengths that are given in the same units, e.g., by using drawings (such as drawings of rulers) and equations with a symbol for the unknown number to represent the problem.

Show your students other ways to solve this same problem. Try a 100-bead rekenrek (photo on page 98). Push 58 beads to the left for the total length of the 2 animals. Then push 22 beads back to the right to subtract the length of the walking stick. How many of the 58 beads are still on the left? Thirty-six—so that's the length in inches of the earthworm.

Number lines that go to 100 work well with these problems, too. Jump from 0 to 22, and mark that for the length of the walking stick. Mark 58 for the total. Demonstrate a counting-up strategy to go from 22 to 58. Jump 10 from 22 to 32; jump another 10 to 42; then jump 10 to 52. Say, "That's 3 tens, or 30. How much farther is it from 52 to 58?" (Hop 6 spaces.) "We jumped 3 tens and 6 ones for a total of 36 inches."

Pairs, Individuals

2.MD.B.5

More Animal Problems

 Actual Size by Steve Jenkins

After you've introduced children to various problem-solving strategies using the book *Actual Size,* leave the book at a center along with hands-on materials for solving a few problems like these written out on cards:

- The giant beetle is 6 inches long. The giant walking stick is 22 inches long. What is their combined length?

- The giant Atlas moth is 12 inches across. The pygmy shrew has a body just 2 inches long. What is the difference in the lengths of these two animals? Use drawings and an equation to show your answer.

- The Goliath frog is 3 feet long. The combined length of the Goliath frog and the saltwater crocodile is 26 feet. How long is the crocodile? Use drawings and an equation to explain your thinking.

Leave some blank index cards at the center so students can write problems for their classmates to solve, based on the information in *Actual Size.*

> ### ✓ QUICK TIP
>
> *See What They Know on page 58 of Operations and Algebraic Thinking is also a great task to use with Standard 2.MD.B.5. It presents a puzzle with paper rulers and asks for proof of a statement.*

Get Up and Go!

 Get Up and Go! by Stuart J. Murphy

Get Up and Go! by Stuart J. Murphy follows a little girl as she gets up in the morning, including the time it takes her to do each step in getting ready to go to school. But wait—this standard isn't about time. It's about number lines! Well, the number line (or time line) in this picture book goes from 0 to 36 minutes, with equally spaced points corresponding to the numbers 1 to 36, so it works for number lines, too. We love to be able to use the same book for multiple standards! The elapsed time activity for this storybook is on pages 127–128.

Make sure each student has a number line. Read the story as a class, and have students track the number of minutes passing by jumping their fingers the number of spaces equal to the minutes that each activity takes. Discuss the sums they are demonstrating as they do this. How many minutes does it take the girl to snuggle Teddy and wash her face? How many minutes does eating breakfast add to that sum?

> ### ✔ QUICK TIP
>
> *We like to use a floor-sized number line from 0 to 30. It is large enough for students to stand on and to add each number by walking or jumping. This provides our vehicle for whole-group exploration with addition and subtraction. Of course, this number line doesn't take us all the way to 100, but maybe you can make one that does!*

Number Line Stories

Provide each student with a number line, and use a class-sized number line for demonstration purposes. Tell stories about life at school, and invite students to follow along on their number lines. Talk about the stories as children use their number lines to solve the sums and differences, as they add and subtract along with the story. Here are two examples, but you can make up your own.

The Art Class: "A class of 21 students is taking an art class. When class is over, 15 students come out of the room right on time. The teacher is waiting in the hallway for the rest of the class. How many students are still in the art room?"

Whole Group

2.MD.B.6 Represent whole numbers as lengths from 0 on a number line diagram with equally spaced points corresponding to the numbers 0, 1, 2, . . . , and represent whole-number sums and differences within 100 on a number line diagram.

Whole Group, Individuals

2.MD.B.6

- Read the story, and then use the number line to solve the problem. Ask one student to point to 21 (or stand on 21 for a floor-sized number line). This stands for the total number of students who were in the art class.

- Ask, "How many students came out right on time?" (15) "How can we show these students leaving the art class? Well, think of 15 as a 10 and a 5. Let's jump back 10 spaces from 21. Where are we?" (11)

- Ask, "Is 11 correct? Is going back 10 spaces enough?" (No, we still have to jump back 5 more, for 5 more students.) "Where are we after jumping back 10, then jumping back 5?" (6) "How many are left in the art room?" (6) The student points to or stands on 6 on the number line.

Going Home: "Now, all 21 children are back in their classroom. Ten children are packed and ready to go home. How many children are not ready?"

- Read the story and have a student stand on 10 on the number line, to represent the 10 students who are ready to go.

- Ask, "How far is 10 from 21, the total number of children in the class? If our person standing on 10 jumps 10 more, then she would be on 20, and 1 more would make the total. $10 + ? = 21$. (11 are not ready.)

This approach is the same as the one for the first story, but think of other ways to show the same problem on the class-sized number line. How about starting at 21 and then counting back 10 ($21 - 10 = ?$). Does this give you the same answer? Sure it does! Encourage your students to show the same problem multiple ways. Doing so increases the depth of their understanding.

Extension: Make a center for number line problems. Start with a 0 to 50 number line; then when the time is right, progress to a number line that goes from 0 to 100. Laminated number lines and dry-erase markers allow for multiple uses. Make up stories based on your school for children to solve at the center. At the end of center time, have students share the different strategies they used.

GRADE 2

Cluster 2.MD.C Work with time and money.

Time Is Passing

 Get Up and Go! by Stuart J. Murphy

C P A
*Whole Group,
Individuals*

2.MD.C.7 Tell and write time from analog and digital clocks to the nearest five minutes, using A.M. and P.M.

You may have used *Get Up and Go!* as a number line story (see page 125). Of course it's also a terrific way to engage students in a discussion about elapsed time. Most second graders know that the way to answer the question "What time is it?" is to read a clock. *Elapsed time* tells how much time has passed, and it involves reading two clock faces. This story provides a good opportunity to use multiple representations to teach time, which is very much in line with the Standards for Mathematical Practices.

The Time Is Passing Data Sheet that we use for this activity has a time line and blank clocks. It's available as a copymaster on page 171. The completed sheet is shown on page 128.

Assign a beginning time of 7:00 A.M., since the story starts early on a school morning. As you read the story, have your students record the time in 4 different ways. As they do, they progress from hands-on to pictorial to abstract.

• Move the hands of a Judy Clock to show the next time in the story (concrete);

• On the data sheet, draw and label the change in time as a jump on the time line, using colors for each jump (pictorial);

• Draw the hands on the analog clock to indicate the correct time (pictorial);

• Write the time in digital form below the clock (abstract).

After the data sheets are completed, use the numbers on the time line to practice mental math. Have children circle the combinations of 10 that they see: 2 and 8, 7 and 3, 6 and 4 to make 30. Then add the 5 and 1 to get the total of 36 minutes elapsed. Is this result the same as the last jump on the time line? Yes!

Math Journal: Have students write the time they get up in the morning two ways—as an analog clock and as a digital clock. Make sure they add A.M. to the digital clock.

Extension: Provide computers so students can practice with the free Elapsed Time interactive from Shodor (www.shodor.org; search for *elapsed time*). Level 1 activities show elapsed time on the hour; level 2 activities provide practice to the 5-minute mark; level 3 goes to the 1-minute mark. Each student can practice at the level that is right for her.

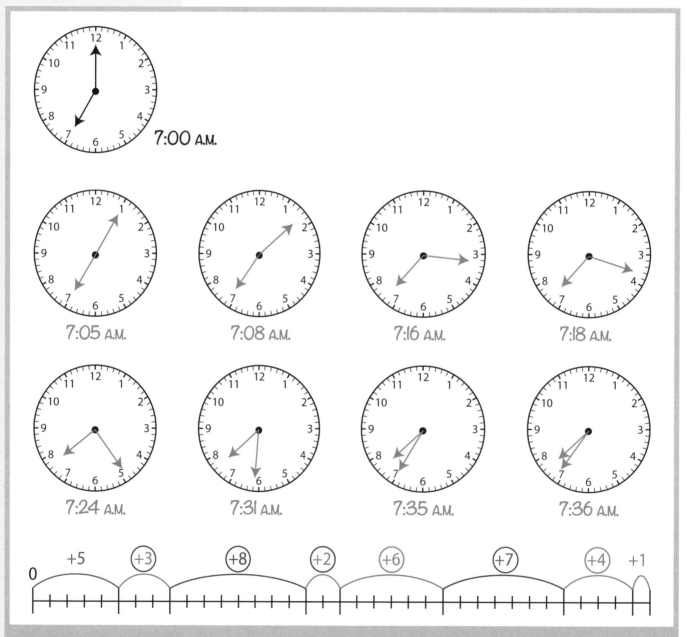

7:00 A.M.

7:05 A.M.   7:08 A.M.   7:16 A.M.   7:18 A.M.

7:24 A.M.   7:31 A.M.   7:35 A.M.   7:36 A.M.

Have students complete the Time Is Passing Data Sheet as you read the book *Get Up and Go!* The data sheet is available as a copymaster on page 171.

Clocks, Clocks, Clocks

 Clocks and More Clocks by Pat Hutchins

Read the book *Clocks and More Clocks*. The book tells the story of Mr. Higgins, who can't figure out why the clocks in his house do not all tell exactly the same time. Which clock is right? As you read, ask children to move the hands on their own practice clocks while you move the hands on the class Judy Clock to match the times in the story. Discuss why the clocks in the different parts of the house don't match. After a few pages your "quick studies" will figure out that all of the clocks are correct. It's just that it takes time for Mr. Higgins to move from room to room. By the time he gets to the next clock, it *looks* like it doesn't match the clock he just left behind. This story will give your students practice telling time to the nearest minute, which is even more precise than the standard requires.

Whole Group

2.MD.C.7

Chimp Time

 Chimp Math: Learning About Time from a Baby Chimpanzee by Ann Whitehead Nagda and Cindy Bickel

This nonfiction book tells the story of Jiggs, a baby chimpanzee who is raised by humans at the zoo where he is born. Time lines, charts, and analog and digital clocks show how often Jiggs is fed through a 24-hour period. Half hours, quarter hours, and time to the nearest 5 minutes are also explored. Start the book as a class read-aloud, and then leave it where children may explore it further.

Whole Group, Individuals

2.MD.C.7

Alexander & His Dollar

 Alexander, Who Used to Be Rich Last Sunday by Judith Viorst

In the classic picture book *Alexander, Who Used to Be Rich Last Sunday*, the title character describes how he frittered away the dollar that his grandparents gave him the previous Sunday. Using real money is a fun way for students to follow the fate of Alexander's wealth while practicing the values of various coins.

Read the story once through for fun. Next, review with students the value of each coin mentioned in the book. As you review, write

Whole Group, Pairs

2.MD.C.8 Solve word problems involving dollar bills, quarters, dimes, nickels, and pennies, using $ and ¢ symbols appropriately. Example: If you have 2 dimes and 3 pennies, how many cents do you have?

the value of each coin where students can see it, using the cent sign (¢). Also be sure to use the dollar sign ($) in the context of Alexander's dollar.

- Give each student (or pair of students) a resealable plastic bag containing 1 dollar as 10 pennies, 10 nickels, and 4 dimes, and a copy of the Alexander & His Dollar worksheet, available on page 172.

- Have children line up their 10 pennies on their worksheets, and count them. Ask, "How much money does 1 penny equal?" (1¢) "How much do these 10 pennies equal?" (10¢) What other coins are worth the same as 10 pennies?" (2 nickels or 1 dime)

- Next, have children line up the 10 nickels. Ask, "What is each nickel worth? (5¢) "So, how should we count nickels?" (by 5s) Count by 5s to find out the value of the nickels. (50¢) Then ask more questions, such as, "What other coins add up to 50 cents (50¢)?" (5 dimes; 10 pennies and 8 nickels; other combinations) "What part of a dollar ($1) do these 10 nickels equal?" (half) "How much are the 10 pennies and the 10 nickels worth together?" (60¢)

- Proceed with the 4 dimes in a similar manner, asking about the value of the coins and how to skip count to find out their value.

Once children are comfortable with the value of the coins, reread the story. As Alexander's money is spent, have students place their real coins on their worksheets next to the item purchased or the amount lost. Ask questions at each stage, for example, "How many different ways can you make 15 cents (15¢) with these coins?" and "How much of one dollar ($1) has Alexander spent so far? Is it more than half, or less than half?" Adjust your questions for the instructional level of your class. Some children will be able to calculate change and decompose numbers, while others will simply count the amount spent or lost.

Counting the value of real coins helps students to illustrate for themselves what happens to Alexander's wealth as the week progresses. The worksheet is available on page 172.

Fill the Pocket

 Alexander, Who Used to Be Rich Last Sunday by Judith Viorst

The title character in *Alexander, Who Used to Be Rich Last Sunday* has his pocket filled by his grandparents. But the money burns a proverbial hole in his pocket, and he soon has nothing left. Fill the Pocket and Burn a Hole in the Pocket are two games related to the book. The games are played in pairs. You may choose to have children make a game board showing Alexander and his pocket. Or, have your students play using any container for the pocket.

- Rules for Fill the Pocket—Play with 10 pennies. Two players take turns placing either 1 coin or 2 coins in Alexander's pocket. No more than 2 coins may be placed on any one turn. As a child places each coin, she must count it and state the total amount in the pocket. The child who places the coin that makes 10 cents wins.

- Burn a Hole in the Pocket is just the opposite. Place any number of coins in Alexander's pocket. Each player takes turns removing either 1 or 2 coins (no more) and stating how much money he took out and how much money is left in the pocket. The player to take out the final coin wins.

Here's an example of how Fill the Pocket might play out. Player A places 1 penny in Alexander's pocket and counts 1 cent. Player B then places 2 pennies and counts 3 cents. Player A then adds 2 cents and counts 5 cents; Player B adds 2 cents and counts 7 cents. Player A can't win at this point. If A adds 1 more penny, B will add 2 pennies and win. If A adds 2 pennies, then B will add 1 penny and win.

Extension: The NCTM Illuminations website has a great interactive lesson, Coin Box (illuminations.nctm.org). Students can count, collect, exchange, and count back change with virtual coins.

DIFFERENTIATING THE GAME

This game is so powerful for differentiation. You can make the amount of money and the variety of coins fit the ability level of your students. Some students will be able to play using all of the coins—pennies, nickels, and dimes—in the Alexander book. Others can manage when quarters are added to the change. Watch students play, and use your observations as formative assessments.

C▸P▸A
Whole Group

2.MD.D.9 Generate measurement data by measuring lengths of several objects to the nearest whole unit, or by making repeated measurements of the same object. Show the measurements by making a line plot, where the horizontal scale is marked off in whole-number units.

GRADE **2**

Cluster 2.MD.D Represent and interpret data.

Pencils by the Dozen

Gather up all the old, used pencils you have on hand, several inch rulers, a yardstick, and a place to write, such as a chalkboard, whiteboard, or easel paper. Then gather the class on the carpet to introduce line plots.

- Say, "We are going to measure these old pencils and plot the findings on a line plot. First let's make the base of the line plot." (Use the yardstick as a guide to draw a horizontal line at the bottom of the board or easel paper.)

- Say, "Along the bottom of the line plot, we need to add numbers to show the lengths in inches of these pencils. But what numbers do we need? How long—or how short—do you think the used pencils are?" (Give children time to discuss how long the used pencils

Variation: Use colored straws cut into various whole-inch lengths. Provide a 1 to 10 number line and have children measure and then plot the straw lengths above the correct numbers on the number line.

might be, and then write the numbers along the bottom of the chart, beneath the line.)

- Next, have 10 volunteers each pick a pencil from the box (10 total) and use the rulers to measure them to the nearest inch. As one student measures her pencil, another student should mark an x above the number that indicates the length of that pencil in inches. Continue until all 10 pencils have been measured.

- Choose another 10 volunteers to measure 10 more pencils. Repeat until the whole box has been measured and plotted.

- Discuss the line plot. Ask, "What do the x's above each number mean?" (Each x stands for 1 pencil that is the length listed below it.) "Did we have any 1-inch pencils? What about 10-inch pencils? Which measurement had the most pencils?"

Math Journal: Provide rulers and a variety of old pencils or crayons for children to measure, as well as 1 to 10 number lines to use for line plots. Have children measure the items and then create a line plot to add to their math journals.

Extension: Repeat the activity, but provide metric rulers and have children measure the pencils to the nearest whole centimeter.

Graphing with Stuart

 Lemonade for Sale by Stuart J. Murphy

Stuart J. Murphy's *Lemonade for Sale* presents a real-world task that involves bar graphs, selling lemonade, a juggler, and repairing a clubhouse—all in the context of an engaging story. Read the story and pose questions along the way. "How many more cups did Stuart and his friends sell on Tuesday than on Monday? How many cups did they sell in the first 3 days combined? What was the difference in sales from Wednesday to Thursday? Why was there a decline in sales? Friday the kids' sales are over the top. Have they earned enough to repair their clubhouse?" (Yes)

Whole Group

2.MD.D.10 Draw a picture graph and a bar graph (with single-unit scale) to represent a data set with up to four categories. Solve simple put-together, take-apart, and compare problems using information presented in a bar graph.

Tiger Graphs

 Tiger Math: Learning to Graph from a Baby Tiger by Ann Whitehead Nagda and Cindy Bickel

T.J., a Siberian tiger, was born at the Denver Zoo. When T.J.'s mother dies, Cindy and the team at the Denver Zoo work to save her baby and keep him healthy. The book provides an engaging, real-world context to teach graphs in a way that leads to deep understanding. Data about T.J.'s progress, and about tigers in general, is provided as circle graphs, bar graphs, and picture graphs. We highly recommend this kid-friendly book that allows children to apply their understanding of graphs. Read sections of the book aloud and display the graphs using a document camera, to introduce each kind of graph in a rich context. Then make the book available at a center for further exploration.

⊙ SEE WHAT THEY KNOW

Use a line plot like the one shown to do a quick check on what your students know and understand. The line plot and discussion prompt are available as a copymaster on page 173.

Heights of Students

```
                 X        X
                 X        X
        X        X        X
        X        X        X        X
 X      X        X        X        X        X        X
 41     42       43       44       45       46       47
```

Height in Inches

Present the line plot and lead a discussion:
"The 18 students in Ms. Lasater's class made the line plot to show their heights in inches. How many students had heights of 43 inches? How about 44 inches? How many students had heights less than 43 inches? Which height is closest to 4 feet? Is this height greater or less than 4 feet? Use drawings, words, and equations to support your answers."

Geometry

Your students come to school with lots and lots of geometric and spatial knowledge. When they were babies, they had shape toys. When they were toddlers, they played with bowls from the lowest kitchen cabinets. And you know that if you give any child a bunch of blocks, that child will start building without any prompting.

The emphasis in primary classrooms must be not just on naming the shapes, but also on recognizing the attributes of those shapes. It isn't enough to be able to say, "This is a square." Students should learn that "This shape has 4 sides and 4 angles. All the sides are the same length, and all the angles are the same size." Terms like *tetrahedron* or *truncated pyramid* are wonderful to say, but if a student does not know what makes a shape a truncated pyramid or a tetrahedron, then he is missing the mathematics.

We also want our students to understand how the attributes of shapes compare and contrast with one another. We want to hear them say, "This square has sides that are the same length as the sides of the triangle. The rectangle and square have right angles. This triangle has one right angle, and this triangle has no right angles." This kind of deep understanding takes time to develop, but with your modeling and their practice, your little charges will become experts at shapes. And when children can correctly apply geometric terms, they're ready for some more serious geometry. So let's give it to them!

Borrow building blocks! Gather pattern blocks! Ask parents for clean containers to stock a "Geometry Museum"! Then use these artifacts for hours of power-packed geometry lessons.

GRADE (K)

Cluster K.G.A Identify and describe shapes (squares, circles, triangles, rectangles, hexagons, cubes, cones, cylinders, and spheres).

K.G.A.1 Describe objects in the environment using names of shapes, and describe the relative positions of these objects using terms such as *above, below, beside, in front of, behind,* and *next to.*

Back-to-Back Pattern Blocks

This game requires children to use correct geometric language and correct positional language. (Positional language is also important in language arts.) Provide at least one pattern block in each shape for each of the students in a pair. You'll need to demonstrate a few times in the beginning, using yourself and a student as the pair.

- Players sit back-to-back on the floor. They decide who will be the leader and who will be the follower.

- The leader uses 5 or 6 pattern blocks to lay out a design that the other person can't see.

- Once the leader has completed the design, he gives directions for the follower. For example, "Start with the orange square. Place the blue diamond above it." The goal is for the follower to build a

In back-to-back pattern blocks, the leader describes the shape to use next, and the follower identifies it. It's fun practice with shapes, and with positional language!

design that matches the leader's design without looking at what the leader has created.

- The follower may stop the leader at any time and ask for clarification.

- Once all directions have been given and followed, both participants slide away and look at their designs. If the directions were given correctly and followed correctly, then the designs should match. Rejoice!

- Switch roles for the next round.

Extension: Once students understand how to do this and know the names of the shapes, challenge them to name a shape without its color. Even more challenging is to *describe* shapes instead of naming them. For example, instead of saying, "Start with the square," the leader would say, "Start with the shape that has 4 sides that are all the same length and 4 corners that are all the same size."

Mystery Bag

Whole Group, Pairs

K.G.A.2 Correctly name shapes regardless of their orientations or overall size.

For this activity, you'll need a mystery bag (a small fabric bag or pillowcase) with some real-world geometric shapes or geometric solids inside—for example, a ball, a small box, a triangle. The idea is for the leader to describe attributes of the shape and for the players to identify what the shape is.

For example, let's say one of those objects is a baseball or some other sphere. First model for students how to describe an object's shape using geometric language:

- Place the bag with its mysterious contents in front of the children.

- Pull out the baseball or other sphere.

- Describe it using geometric language, for example, "This baseball has no points, no faces, and no edges."

- Return the baseball or other sphere to the bag.

- Repeat for the other objects in the bag.

Next, invite the children to play the game. Ask one child to reach into the mystery bag and grab an object—but to keep it hidden in

the bag. The child describes the shape's attributes, using geometric language. The other children listen to the clues and identify the shape. The first child to give the correct answer is the next one to reach into the mystery bag and give new clues.

Math Journal: Have children write or draw clues to describe the shape of something you would find in a grocery store.

Everyone loves a mystery! Children identify a shape by touch, then describe its attributes well enough that others know what it is without hearing its name.

Whole Group

K.G.A.2

Shape Collage Posters

Your students will add to these posters from the moment you hang them up until you decide it's time to take them down. Make blank posters with the names of geometric shapes that students should focus on—for example, you could start with three posters labeled Triangles, Rectangles, and Circles. Then hand out scissors, old magazines, and old newspapers, and ask your students to go on a shape scavenger hunt. They should cut out any pictures of objects with these shapes, and then glue each picture onto the correct poster. Encourage your students to continue this hunt at home by searching through any printed materials they have that may be cut.

As the posters become a fixture in your classroom, ask your kiddos to add more words and labels to the posters. For example, "3 sides, 3 corners, 3 angles" and "shaped like an A" work nicely on the triangle poster.

Shape Sort

Pairs

Gather lots of clean, empty boxes, jars, and other containers, or use the shapes in the Geometry Museum suggested on page 135. Also collect, or make out of card stock, a number of large, flat shapes. Then set up a sorting center with two clearly defined areas that can hold the items—you might use two hula-hoops or a piece of tape to divide a tabletop in two. Label one area Flat, 2-D and the other Solid, 3-D. Partners take turns picking up a shape, discussing if it is 3-D or 2-D, and then placing that shape in the correct set. The next pair of students can check the newly created sets before removing them and sorting them again.

Math Journal: Ask children to record the two sets they created using labeled pictures.

K.G.A.3 Identify shapes as two-dimensional (lying in a plane, "flat") or three-dimensional ("solid").

GRADE Ⓚ

Cluster K.G.B Analyze, compare, create, and compose shapes.

Geometry Slide

Whole Group, Small Groups, Pairs

Set up a geometry slide center. Use a stack of books to prop up one end of a piece of wood. (A loose shelf works well for this.) Make three simple signs out of index cards, one each for Roll, Tumble, and Slide. You'll also need some three-dimensional shapes, such as clean cans, boxes, and plastic jars. Once everything is set up, introduce the activity:

- Hold up each sign and review the meanings of Roll, Tumble, and Slide with your students. Then place the signs on the table to the side of the slide.

- Model what to do. Hold a cylinder lengthwise at the top of the slide.

- Ask the children, "I'm going to let go of this cylinder at the top of this geometry slide. Do you think it will slide, roll, or tumble down to the floor?"

- Allow discussion and predictions.

K.G.B.4 Analyze and compare two- and three-dimensional shapes, in different sizes and orientations, using informal language to describe their similarities, differences, parts (e.g., number of sides and vertices/"corners") and other attributes (e.g., having sides of equal length).

• Let the cylinder roll to the bottom. Tell the children, "It rolled. I'm going to put it over here by the Roll sign. Now, I'm going to test another object."

After you've modeled what to do, invite children to come to the slide in pairs or small groups during centers time. Let them test the three-dimensional objects to see how they move down the slide. Remind them to pay close attention to what makes some shapes roll, some slide, and some tumble, and to notice if any shapes move differently depending on how they are placed.

Remind students to return the shapes to the same place after they have tested them, so their classmates may do the same tests.

Math Journal: Have students record which shapes slid, which ones rolled, and which ones tumbled, and why. They may draw the shapes or write about them.

Variation: Ask your students to think of another way to sort the shapes, such as number of sides (faces) or number of corners (vertices). Encourage children who can write to make their own labels. Students can also ask friends to look at their sets and figure out the rule that was used to sort the objects.

C ▸ P ▸ A

*Small Groups,
Pairs, Individuals*

K.G.B.5 Model shapes in the world by building shapes from components (e.g., sticks and clay balls) and drawing shapes.

Building Buildings

Remember the boxes, cans, and jars you gathered for the Geometry Museum (page 135) or for Shape Sort and Geometry Slide (page 139)? Once your students are done sorting, sliding, and rolling them, it is time to use those materials to build buildings, people, or robots. An adult with a glue gun (or patient children with liquid glue) can attach smaller boxes and cones into complex shapes to compose larger three-dimensional figures that mimic those in the real world. In our many years of teaching, we have seen the creation of cities, homes, and a robot village from the well-used geometric shapes. An open house for parents celebrating the completion of the Geometry Town complete with children's rich vocabulary and enthusiasm, is a guaranteed success story!

Have your students build model items from the real world or from the imagination, using component shapes.

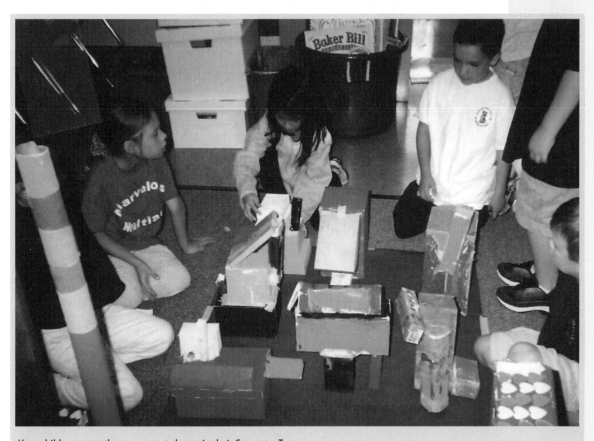

Have children name the component shapes in their Geometry Town.

Individuals

K.G.B.5

Face It!

While your students are building buildings, have them select a few three-dimensional shapes, place one face of each shape on paper, and trace around it with a pencil. You can also provide wooden or plastic three-dimensional solids for them to trace. After each student is finished tracing, have her write the name of the two-dimensional shape she created from the three-dimensional shape.

Pairs

K.G.B.5

Tower Building

For this activity, your students will need cans, boxes, and other containers brought in from home, as well as space to work on a table or floor. If you assembled a Geometry Museum (page 135), then let students use those materials.

Begin by announcing, "You and a friend may work together to try to build the tallest tower in the class, using these boxes and containers that everyone has brought in. You may want to measure your tower once it is built. But here are the rules. You need to share the boxes and containers with your classmates. You may not stand on a chair or desk or table. You must use quiet inside voices. When I say 'clean up,' you have to return all of the materials."

Allow children to build, and create, and have a great time. With each attempt at stacking, whether or not it succeeds, they are beginning to understand and internalize the properties of geometric solids.

How you have your students measure their towers once they've built them depends on their ages and abilities. The simplest approach is to have them "eyeball" the structures and compare the height of one to the height of another. You could also have them comment on how tall a tower is compared to the height of one child: "Wow! This tower is as tall as Scott's shoulder!" or "Look! This tower comes to Robert's waist!" If any children are ready to use units of measure, have them measure a tower using a meterstick or yardstick.

Math Journal: Say to students, "Record what you have learned about building with geometric shapes. Then draw your tallest tower. Label the shapes you used in that tower, if you can."

Pattern Block Power

C P A

Individuals

Using pattern blocks, children can explore the many shapes they can create by combining other shapes. Encourage your students to explore the shapes they can make. Here are some suggestions:

- Two square pattern blocks placed side by side form a rectangle, while 3 squares in a row make a longer rectangle. But 4 square pattern blocks arranged with 2 in the top row and 2 in the bottom row make another square!

- Two equilateral triangles put together can make a rhombus.

- Ask your students questions like, "Can you build a bigger square using 8 squares? How about using 9 squares? How many triangles do you need to build another triangle?" This should inspire them to discover more shapes they can make from smaller ones.

Math Journal: Ask your charges to trace around the pattern blocks on paper to record their favorite larger shape and the smaller shapes that make it up, and record this as a journal entry.

K.G.B.6 Compose simple shapes to form larger shapes. *For example, "Can you join these two triangles with full sides touching to make a rectangle?"*

QUICK TIP

It is important that we use correct mathematical language with children. Although students are using pattern blocks, they are forming designs, not patterns. A design is finite, while a pattern continues.

Composing shapes with pattern blocks; in this example, two equilateral triangles make a rhombus; a rhombus and a triangle make a trapezoid; two trapezoids make a hexagon.

Small Groups

K.G.B.6

Street Scene of 2-D Shapes

Assign a team of 3 to 4 children to create a two-dimensional streetscape of houses. They should build the streetscape using squares, rectangles, and triangles of all sizes cut from wrapping paper, wallpaper, sandpaper, and construction paper. (You may either cut all paper ahead of time, or let the children cut the shapes.) Have students mount their buildings on poster board to create a street scene and then write about their street.

This activity encourages your kids to "make a scene" with shapes!

 SEE WHAT THEY KNOW

What have your kindergartners learned about composing new shapes? Find out by gathering small groups, giving them some pattern blocks, and seeing how they approach the following problem.

"Clare and Ed are playing with the green triangles from the pattern block tub. Clare has composed a rhombus from the triangles, and Ed has made a trapezoid. Is this possible? If you said yes, show me how Clare and Ed made these shapes using only green triangles."

GRADE ①

Cluster 1.G.A Reason with shapes and their attributes.

Name It!

This activity lets children uncover what makes a shape, a shape. Give your children pattern blocks, tiles, paper cutouts, pictures from magazines, containers brought from home, and anything else you can find that has a shape. This activity can be done and redone several times because the rule for finding a certain shape can change. The following rules for two-dimensional shapes will keep your geometry geniuses busy over several days:

- Which shapes have 3 sides (or 4 sides, 5 sides, 6 sides)?

- Which shapes have 3 angles (or 4 angles, 5 angles, 6 angles)?

- Which of these 4-angled shapes has sides all the same length?

- Which shapes have curves but no angles?

Discuss the shapes that go together based on these rules. Ask about attributes that do not have to do with shape. For example, hold up a red square and a red triangle and ask, "Are these the same shape? Why not? They are the same color. Why aren't they the same shape?" Let students figure out for themselves what attributes define and identify a shape.

Extension: Have your students sort three-dimensional shapes. Use rules such as, "These shapes have circle bases" and "These shapes have square faces."

***Whole Group,
Small Groups, Pairs***

> **1.G.A.1** Distinguish between defining attributes (e.g., triangles are closed and three-sided) versus non-defining attributes (e.g., color, orientation, overall size); build and draw shapes to possess defining attributes.

1.G.A.2 Compose two-dimensional shapes (rectangles, squares, trapezoids, triangles, half-circles, and quarter-circles) or three-dimensional shapes (cubes, right rectangular prisms, right circular cones, and right circular cylinders) to create a composite shape, and compose new shapes from the composite shape.

Space Shapes

Captain Invincible and the Space Shapes by Stuart J. Murphy

The book *Captain Invincible and the Space Shapes* abounds with three-dimensional shapes: cubes, right rectangular prisms, right circular cones, and right circular cylinders found with every turn of the page. This activity uses Polydrons and part of the *Captain Invincible* story to help children explore all the attributes of a cube. Provide a tub of Polydrons for each small group of students.

As the story begins, Captain Invincible and his space dog, Comet, are trying to escape a meteor shower. They are using space shapes on the ship's control panel to save themselves and their spaceship. Comet has to identify and select the cube for the job at hand. Read the story up to this point and then lead a discussion along the following lines.

Polydrons are flat, regular shapes that can be connected into two- or three-dimensional shapes. These girls have made a net for a cube using Polydrons.

These girls have folded their Polydron net into a cube. If you do not have Polydrons, cut tagboard squares and let pairs of children tape them into a net and then into a cube.

- "How does Comet know which shape is the cube? Let's build cubes with our Polydrons so we can explore a cube and its attributes."

- Show a cube you've made and say, "Look at the cube I have made. How many squares did I use? How many squares will you need to make a cube?" Give children time to make cubes.

- Now return to the story. Turn to the page with the cube sending out radar beams to find a pathway to safety. Ask, "What does Captain Invincible say about the cube that you have already discovered? That's right, a cube has 6 sides."

Explore more of this delightful book and use it for building, discussing, and mastering the other three-dimensional shapes noted in this standard. Enjoy!

Individuals

1.G.A.2

Geometry Art

Any artist knows that everyday objects, including animals, are made of basic shapes. These three projects—making a pig, a turkey, or a kitty cat—let your students practice geometry and art at the same time. The projects also require children to read along and follow directions. So, is this project art, math, or reading? The answer to all three is, "Yes!"

Copymasters of instructions for all three projects are available at the back of this book:

- Pigometry, making a pig, page 174

- Geome-turkey, making a turkey, page 175

- Geome-kitty, making a kitty cat, page 176

Choose one project for all of your students, so that all children are following the same directions. This reduces confusion and helps students to focus on the shapes. In addition to the copymasters, students also need glue, scissors, straightedges, and a selection of colored construction paper. You may also wish to provide objects that they can trace around for drawing circles, triangles, and rectangles. Hand out the materials and instructions, and celebrate the diversity of results!

The best part about these art projects is that even though everyone follows the same directions, all the pigs, turkeys, and kitties look different, just like the children do!

A House for a Mouse

 Town Mouse and Country Mouse, any version

Read one of the many versions of Town Mouse and Country Mouse, based on the ancient tale attributed to Aesop. Cut paper in a variety of colors before you begin, as described in the Art Tip box. Tell your students you want to create a village of country homes for town mice to visit when they need to escape the city. Lead the construction—and the discussion of geometry—while your students assemble the houses.

> ## ART TIP
>
> *Cut the construction paper shapes before beginning. Use a variety of colors.*
>   *Each mouse house needs:*
> * *One 4 × 17-inch strip for the walls*
> * *One 6 × 12-inch piece for the roof*
> * *Several 1 × 1-inch or 1 × 2-inch pieces for the windows*
>   *Put out some additional paper for options like chimneys or trees. Students also need tape or glue, scissors, and markers.*

* Begin with the 4 × 17-inch paper strip. Say that this will be the walls of the mouse house. Discuss that this shape is a rectangle with 4 sides and 4 corners, which mathematicians call *angles*. There are 2 pairs of *congruent* sides. *Congruent* sides all have the same length.

* Once you have milked the geometry of the long rectangle for all it's worth, start the construction. Ask children to fold over a tab on one of the shorter sides to "about the length from the tip of your thumb to the knuckle" (or about 1 inch). (That tab will later be glued under the other end of the rectangle.) Ask, "What shape do you have now?" (It is still a rectangle.)

* Hold the rectangle horizontally, so that it is 16 inches wide, keeping the tab folded under. Say, "Fold your long rectangle in half so that the two bottom angles meet and the two top angles meet." Demonstrate that the wide long rectangle is being folded in half with a vertical fold. Ask, "What shape do we have now? How large is it compared to the first shape?" (This is still a rectangle, but it is half the size of the rectangle that was folded.)

- Open your folded rectangle and ask, "How many halves make the whole rectangle?" (Two; close the rectangle at the fold before continuing.)

- Say, "Now take the half-rectangles and fold them in half again so that the bottom angles meet and the top angles meet." Ask, "What shape is this? How large is it compared with the first shape?" (The shape should look close to a square. It is one-fourth the size of the first rectangle.)

> ✓ **QUICK TIP**
>
> *The Southwest Geometry activity (page 156) is another good one for exploring fractions of a shape.*

- Encourage discussion about how the square is still a rectangle, and it is one-fourth the size of the first rectangle. Ask kids to open their folded rectangles to count the smaller squares using the folds as the lines. Point out that when a shape is divided into equal parts, all of the fractional parts are equal to each other.

- After a good discussion of the geometry, tell children it is time to cut a door. Demonstrate how to cut a vertical slit up the center of one of the squares and a horizontal slit across.

- Show students how to re-fold the paper so that it forms a square when placed on an end. Glue or tape the 1-inch tab to the adjacent wall.

- For the roof, fold a piece of 6 × 12-inch paper in half to make a tent-like roof. Attach it with tape.

- Have children glue small precut rectangles (1 × 1 inch or 1 × 2 inches) to make one window for each wall without a door. Challenge children to use crayons to divide one window into halves, one window into fourths, and one window into thirds.

- As time allows, let children decorate their homes. Assemble all homes together to create a cozy village for the city mice.

Mouse houses are made by folding long rectangles into 4 smaller squares. The finished houses are about 4 inches wide and 4 inches deep, with walls 4 inches high, plus the roof.

Architecture Center

Tell families that you're collecting postcards and pictures of buildings and artwork that show geometry. Display the pictures that the children bring in at a center. Ask children to write or tell you about the geometry they see in the buildings. Have them compare the shapes in the pictures to other shapes they've been exploring in the classroom, such as those in a Geometry Museum you may have set up (page 135).

An architecture center gets families involved and kids intrigued.

I am looking at the picture of Washington D.C. and I see squares in the windows, cylinders in the pillars and the doors look like really tall rectangles. I think there are triangles over the windows too.

Students observe photos of buildings and learn to recognize geometric shapes in the world around them.

👁 SEE WHAT THEY KNOW

Pose this problem for your students and see how they solve it. You may read the problem to the children, or use the copymaster on page 177. If you use this as an independent task, first be sure that your students can read the directions and understand the task. Provide 2 paper plates and a marker or scissors, and then read the problem.

"Mom ordered two medium pizzas for the family. She cut one pizza into 2 equal pieces. She cut the other pizza into 4 equal pieces. Show Mom's cuts. You may cut the plates or draw lines on them." Give children time to do this, and then say: "Mom gave Bill 2 pieces. She gave Pat 1 piece. Both think the shares are fair. Can you show me which piece or pieces each person has?" When they have done so, ask, "Can you show me 2 pieces that are not fair shares?"

GRADE ②

Cluster 2.G.A Reason with shapes and their attributes.

2.G.A.1 Recognize and draw shapes having specified attributes, such as a given number of angles or a given number of equal faces. Identify triangles, quadrilaterals, pentagons, hexagons, and cubes.

Giraffe

This activity provides an opportunity to practice reading and following directions, as well as drawing shapes and measuring—so many standards being addressed in one fun art project!

Make copies of the instruction sheet How to Create a Splendid Giraffe on page 178. Also give students pencils, inch rulers, tape or glue, and sheets of brown, yellow, tan, and orange paper.

As a class, read aloud and follow the numbered steps for measuring and cutting the shapes, and then assemble them into a giraffe. Stop to discuss the defining attributes of each shape as you draw it. Pattern blocks may be helpful for drawing some hexagonal spots.

Variation: If any of your students are able to read and understand the directions on their own, then this would be a great time to differentiate. Let them complete the activity independently.

Discuss the attributes of the shapes that make up each happy giraffe.

Pattern-Block Bugs

Put containers of pattern blocks where groups of children can reach them. Have them make "bugs" using the pattern block shapes or paper cutouts. Encourage them to trace around the shapes to capture the bugs on paper and then color them.

Next, ask them to write all about their bug creatures. Prompt them with ideas for writing by asking questions like the following: "What are the attributes of your bug? What shapes did you use to make your bug? Name each of these shapes. How many sides and angles does each of these shapes have?"

Variation: Got computers? After a child has created a pattern-block bug, send him to the NCTM Dynamic Paper interactive (illuminations.nctm.org; click on Activities and then Dynamic Paper). He can draw, print, color, and cut out the shapes he needs for his bug from Dynamic Paper.

Extension: Use Polydrons (photos on pages 146–147) to build cubes that resemble the boxes used to observe real bugs that we catch. Ask students, "How many faces does your bug cube have? How many edges do you count?"

Windows & Rectangles

C ▸ P ▸ A

Whole Group,
Small Groups

2.G.A.2 Partition a rectangle into rows and columns of same-size squares and count to find the total number of them.

 Bigger, Better, Best! by Stuart J. Murphy

Bigger, Better, Best! follows the adventures of three siblings as they explore their new house and argue about "whose is biggest." Distribute 1-inch tiles to your students so that, as you read, they can mimic the children in the story as they partition their windows (rectangles) using same-size squares to settle the argument of "whose window is bigger."

- Have children start by building Jeff's window, which is 3 squares tall and 4 squares wide. Ask how many total squares they used to tile the area. (12)

- Take this concrete activity to the pictorial level using 1-inch grid paper. Have children draw the 3-square by 4-square window on the grid paper, and then count the squares.

Tiles help students design windows for the characters in the book *Bigger, Better, Best!*

- Use a document camera to show the class the picture of Jenny's window. Ask a student to describe the shape of her window (only 2 squares high, but 6 squares wide).

- Break into small groups to build Jenny's window using tiles. Have each group draw a picture of the tile rectangle for Jenny's window on the 1-inch grid paper. Ask, "How many squares is Jenny's window?" (12) "Whose window is bigger?" (They are the same size.) "How do you know?" (They take the same number of squares.)

- Have all of the children visit the other groups to compare findings, and then meet again as a large group to discuss results.

- Ask children to design, then draw, two different windows for Jenny and Jeff that take up the same amount of space in tiles (use the same number of tiles) but have different arrangements of tiles. For example, one window could be 4 tiles wide and 4 tiles tall, while the other is 8 tiles wide and 2 tiles tall.

◉ SEE WHAT THEY KNOW

Find out how your students are thinking about the shapes of equal shares of identical wholes. Provide some 1-inch tiles and either read the problem below, or make copies of the problem as it appears on page 179. If you do this as an independent task, first make sure that your students can read the problem independently.

"John has 13 square tiles. He says he can make 3 different rectangles with these 13 tiles. He will use all 13 tiles in each rectangle. Vivian disagrees. She thinks John can make only 1 rectangle. He could turn that rectangle different ways, but it would still just be 1 long, skinny rectangle. Who do you think is correct and why? Vivian also tells John that if he uses only 12 of his squares, he could make many different rectangular shapes. How many different rectangles can you make with 12 square tiles?"

Paper Plate Fractions

Paper plates from a dollar store are a kid-friendly tool for showing circles in wholes, halves, and fourths. We like to use three different plate colors for this activity: yellow plates for the whole; red plates cut into 2 congruent pieces for the halves; and blue plates cut into 4 congruent pieces for the fourths.

Hand out some plates and plate pieces so that each table has some of each color and shape. Allow time for exploration. Then begin the rich discussion.

2.G.A.3 Partition circles and rectangles into two, three, or four equal shares, describe the shares using the words *halves, thirds, half of, a third of,* etc., and describe the whole as two halves, three thirds, four fourths. Recognize that equal shares of identical wholes need not have the same shape.

- Ask, "Can you hold up one whole paper plate?"

- Continue, "Look at the red pieces. How many red pieces does it take to cover the yellow whole plate?" Allow children time to discover this.

- Reinforce, "The red piece is 1 half of the whole. It takes 2 halves to make a whole."

- Continue, "Now look at the blue pieces. Are they the same shape as the red pieces? What do you notice? How many blue pieces does it take to make a whole?"

- Say, "Since 4 equal pieces make a whole, and 4 blue pieces make a whole, we call this fraction a fourth. It takes 4 fourths to make a whole."

These paper plate fraction tools can be one of your "go-to" tools for the rest of the school year, whenever there are queries or problems involving fractions.

Extension: Fill your math center with paper plate fractions, circle cut-outs, and fraction pictures. The book *Ed Emberley's Picture Pie: A Cut and Paste Drawing Book* has a variety of examples of wholes, halves, and fourths of a circle being used to make beautiful butterflies, flowers, fish, and other objects. Once students have the idea, the possibilities are endless.

Paper plates of the same diameter in wholes, halves, and fourths are an easy, inexpensive tool for exploring fractions.

Southwest Geometry

 Coyote Steals the Blanket: A Ute Tale by Janet Stevens

Read the book *Coyote Steals the Blanket: A Ute Tale* to your class. This book is based on a folktale, which has been retold and illustrated by Janet Stevens. The story involves Coyote's desert encounters with a hummingbird, a mountain goat, and a bighorn sheep. Unfortunately for Coyote, he ignores the hummingbird's directions and steals a beautiful Native American woven blanket. What happens next explains why, to this day, coyotes are always racing around, never sitting still.

After reading the story, we implore students to create a blanket for Coyote so he can return the one he stole. This is the hook, and they always go for it!

To make the blanket, each child will need one 8-inch square of gray paper and four 4-inch squares of paper in yellow, green, red, blue, black, or white—colors commonly found in Native American weaving. Tell the students, "You need to select any 4 colors from these choices. Make sure you choose 4 *different* colors."

Ask each child to place her 4 small squares on her 1 large square. Talk about how all 4 squares cover the 1 large square, so each of the small squares is 1/4 the size of the large square. Tell the children that the 4 squares are *congruent* to each other because they have the same shape and size. Tell them that the 1 large square is *similar* to the smaller squares. *Similar* shapes have the same shape but a different size. Reinforce the concept that all squares are similar to all other squares.

Now ask your students to take off 1 square. Say, "There are 4 colors: 1/4 of the colors is missing, but 3/4 of the colors are still there. So 3/4 of the large square is still covered."

Remove another square and describe what is happening: "Two of the squares are missing, so 1/2 of the square is gray and 1/2 of the square is covered with colors."

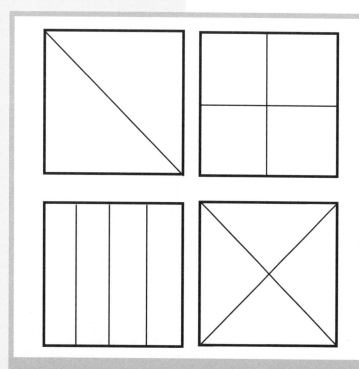

Have students fold and cut each of their 4 small squares as shown. Each child should end up with 2 large triangles, 4 rectangles, 4 squares, and 4 small triangles.

Even though each student uses just 4 colors, make all 6 colors available for students to choose from. That way, your finished class blanket will be more colorful.

Then ask your students to remove one more square and discuss how 1/4 of the large square is covered in a color and 3/4 of the square is now gray. Whenever possible, point out that the fraction pairs you are talking about (1/4 and 3/4, or 1/2 and 1/2) always total 1 whole.

Next, have students fold and cut their small squares as shown on page 156 . As they are folding and cutting, emphasize that they are folding each square into fourths. Yes, even though the shapes that they cut from the squares are different, each shape equals 1/4 of the total square!

After children have cut their squares, have them arrange the shapes on top of their gray square so that no gray is showing and no pieces are hanging over the edges. Give students time to move and re-move pieces. This is good practice for them. Once they've got all the pieces in place, have them glue the pieces to the gray paper.

Follow up by arranging the large squares into a class blanket. Cut some black paper into a fringe, add it to the outside edges, and admire your complete "blanket"!

C P A
Whole Group,
Pairs, Individuals

2.G.A.3

Fractions from Rectangles

Geoboards provide an excellent way for young children to make rectangles of various sizes and divide them to show equal parts. Distribute geoboards and bands to students. While they manipulate the geoboards and bands, lead the discussion along these lines. Say, "Use one color of band to show a rectangle. Now, divide the rectangle in half using a different colored band. Show your rectangle to your partner." Ask several children to share their divided rectangles with the group. Ask, "Has this student attended to precision? Is the rectangle divided in 2 equal parts?"

Continue, this time using thirds. Ask, "Can you make a rectangle with one color of band and divide it into 3 equal pieces using 2 bands of another color?" This may be harder for some children than for others. Have students share different ways they achieved dividing the rectangle into 3 equal parts.

When you move on to fourths, give the students a couple of examples, and then let them explore. Encourage, "Four equal parts may be shown with a long rectangle divided into 4 equal pieces, or by a square with 1 horizontal line and 1 vertical line that divide the square into 4 smaller squares. Can you think of another way to show 4 equal parts, one that makes different shapes?"

Geoboards are great tools for exploring how to divide shapes into equal parts.

Copymasters & Patterns

Coloring Book Page 3 *Use with Coloring Book, page 35.*

Coloring Book Page 4 *Use with Coloring Book, page 35.*

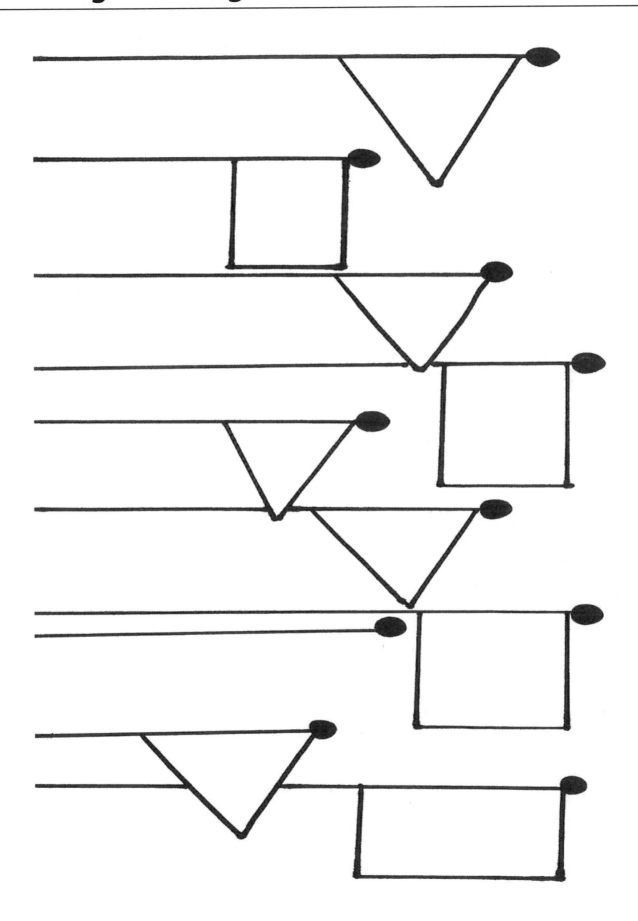

Rocket Storyboard Pattern *Use with Rocket Science, page 35.*

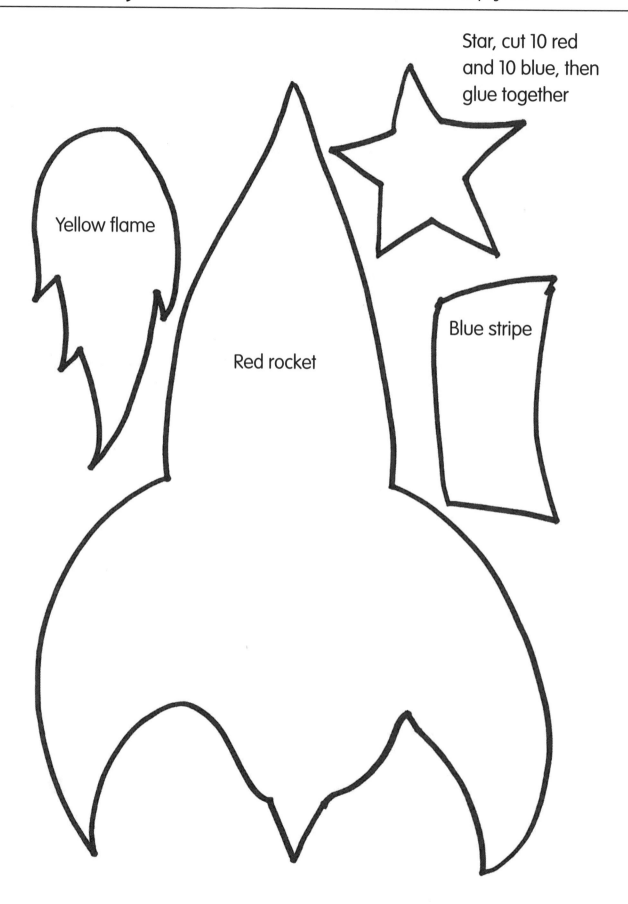

Star, cut 10 red and 10 blue, then glue together

Yellow flame

Red rocket

Blue stripe

Butterfly Storyboard Pattern *Use with Butterfly Storyboard, page 36.*

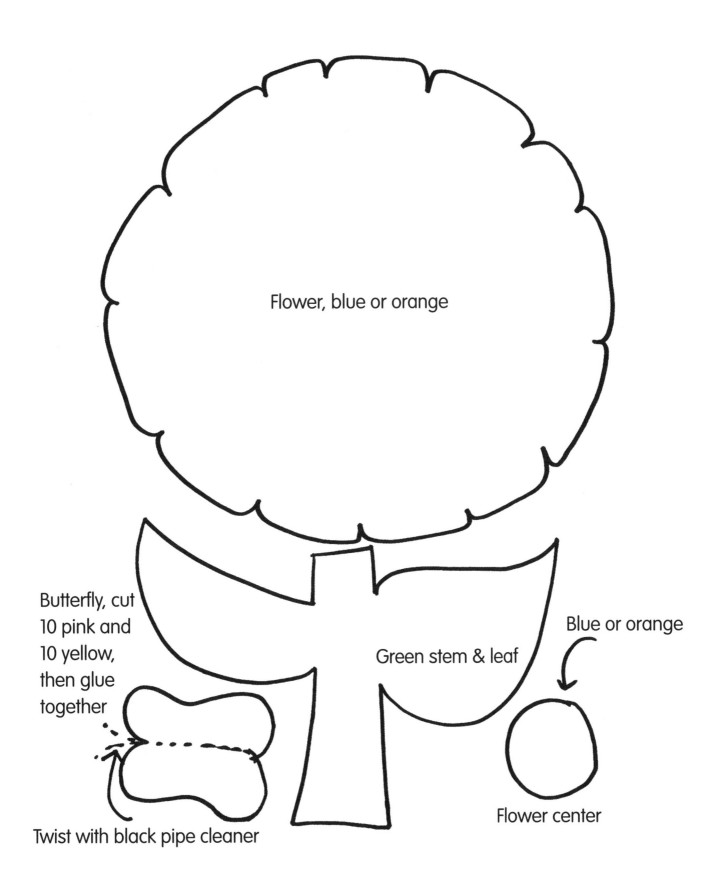

Flower, blue or orange

Butterfly, cut 10 pink and 10 yellow, then glue together

Green stem & leaf

Blue or orange

Twist with black pipe cleaner

Flower center

Bear & Buzzy Bee Storyboard Pattern *Use with Bear & Buzzy Bee*
Storyboard, page 36.

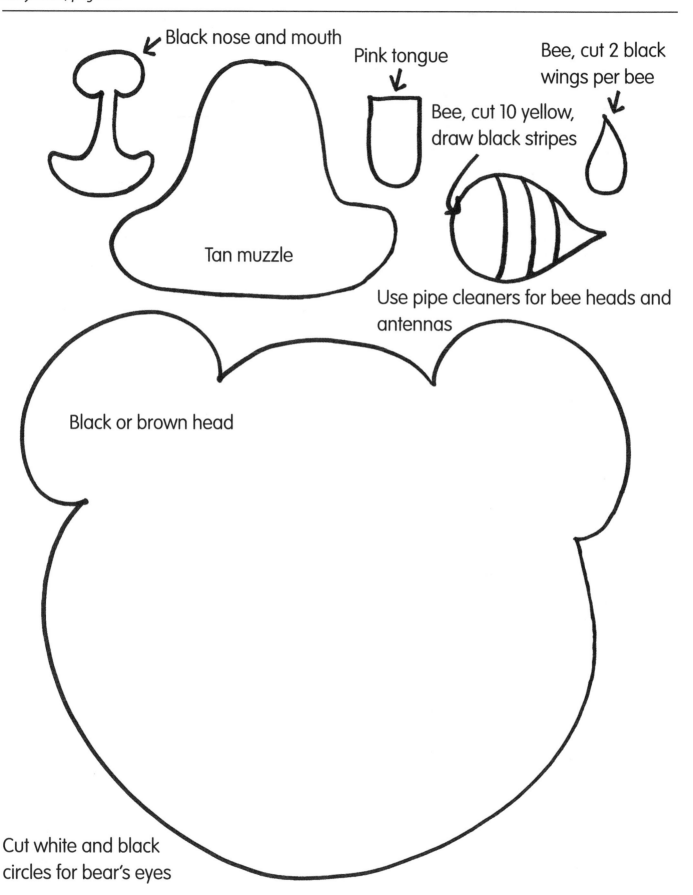

Black nose and mouth

Pink tongue

Bee, cut 2 black wings per bee

Bee, cut 10 yellow, draw black stripes

Tan muzzle

Use pipe cleaners for bee heads and antennas

Black or brown head

Cut white and black circles for bear's eyes

Spaces for Ten Storyboard Pattern *Use with Spaces for Ten, page 37.*

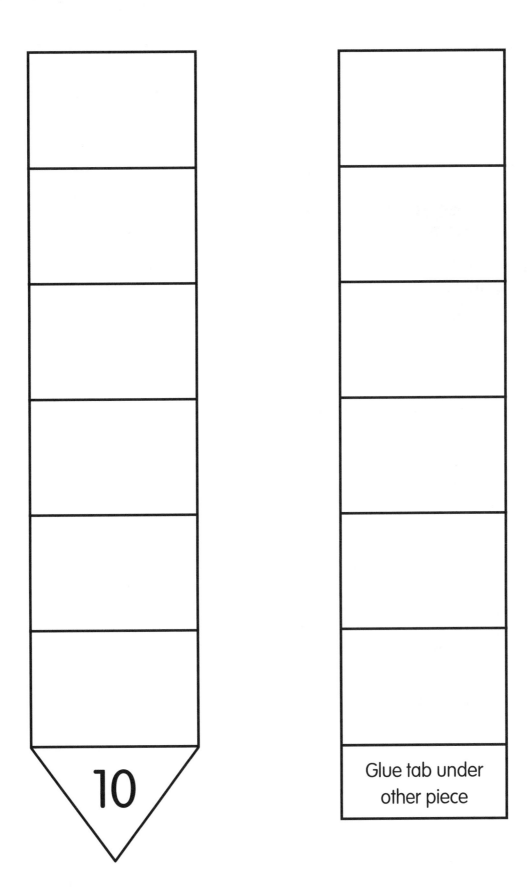

10

Glue tab under
other piece

Here's an example of the kind of open-ended task that you can use to assess how your first graders are doing at developing rich problem-solving skills. Provide paper, pencils or crayons, and 10 small objects; real acorns are nice, but any small objects will work. First, read the story aloud. Discuss what the math problem is, in the story. Once you are sure that the children understand the words and the task, let them work on it in pairs, small groups, or alone. Be sure to celebrate the different ways your students solve this problem.

- -

Acorn Problem

Mama Squirrel has a chore for Little Squirrel to do each day. Mama has hollowed out many holes in the tree to store nuts for the winter. Little Squirrel has to fill one hole each day. Each hole is large enough to store 10 nuts. Little Squirrel finds 3 nuts by the sidewalk, 4 nuts under the big oak tree, and 2 nuts on the roof.

Does he have enough to fill the hole? _____

If not, how many more nuts does he need? _____

Use pictures and words to show your thinking.

___ I did this with my class.   ___ I did this with a group.   ___ I did this on my own.

This task works well as an independent assessment, a small group task, or a class task where discussion is practiced. If you use this as an independent task, first be sure that your students can read the directions and understand the task. You want this math task to require mathematical thinking and not be hindered by readability.

- -

Ruler Dilemma

John has cut two strips of paper. One strip is 12 inches long and the other strip is 10 inches long. Judd says that he can cut 1 inch off of each strip, and the two strips will still have a difference of 2 inches. John does not believe this. He thinks that cutting off 2 inches will make one strip 4 inches longer than the other.

Who is right? _____

Why is he right? Use pictures, equations, and words to prove your answer. You may also use Unifix cubes, rulers, or any other classroom materials to show your work.

____ I did this with my class.   ____ I did this with a group.   ____ I did this on my own.

Here's a problem you can use to uncover your students' thinking processes. Choose the format that works best for your students: reading the question aloud to the class or to small groups, copying and distributing it for independent use, or another approach. Provide some base-10 blocks so you can observe how students are solving the problem.

- -

Row Past 100 Problem

Jennifer and Doris are playing Row Past 100 using base-10 blocks. Doris rolls +100 three times and −100 once. Jennifer rolls +100 two times, +10 nine times, and −100 once.

Doris claims that she has the higher number. Jennifer disagrees; she thinks she has the higher number.

Who is correct? _____

Can you show who is correct using base-10 blocks? Draw your blocks.

___ I did this with my class.   ___ I did this with a group.   ___ I did this on my own.

Time Is Passing Data Sheet Use with Time Is Passing, page 127.

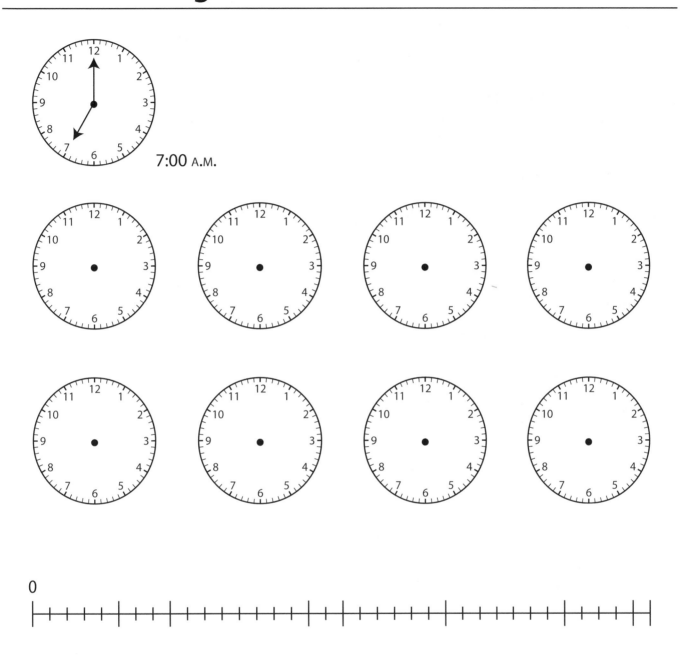

7:00 A.M.

0

Alexander & His Dollar *Use with Alexander & His Dollar, page 129.*

Item	Money Spent
Bubble Gum	
Breath, Jump, & Marble Bets	
Rent-a-Snake	
Bad Words Fine	
Toilet and Floor Crack	
Chocolate Candy	
Magic Trick	
Kicking	
Garage Sale	

You Need:

10 Pennies	10 Nickels	4 Dimes

MD: Grade 2 See What They Know *Use with page 134.*

For this formative assessment, choose the format that works best for observing how your students approach solving the problem: whole class or small groups with teacher support, or independent. If you use this as an independent task, first be sure that your students can read the directions and understand the task. You want to see how your students think mathematically, without anyone being hindered by readability.

Student Heights

Heights of Students

```
                    X       X
                    X       X
            X       X       X
            X       X       X       X
    X       X       X       X       X       X       X
   ───────────────────────────────────────────────────
    41      42      43      44      45      46      47
```

Height in Inches

The 18 students in Ms. Lasater's class made the line plot to show their heights in inches. Use the line plot to answer the following questions. Use drawings, words, and equations to support your answers.

How many students had a height of 43 inches? _____

How many students had a height of 44 inches? _____

How many students had a height less than 43 inches? _____

Which height is closest to 4 feet? _____

Is this height greater or less than 4 feet? _____

___ I did this with my class.   ___ I did this with a group.   ___ I did this on my own.

173

Pigometry
Use with Geometry Art, page 148.

Oink! Oink! Follow these directions to make a pig.

1. Choose black, pink, or gray paper for each body part.

2. Cut 7 similar circles for the head, eyes, body, snout, and nostrils.

3. Cut 2 congruent triangles for ears.

4. Cut 4 congruent rectangles for legs.

5. Glue all the pieces together to assemble one fabulous pig.

6. Twirl a pipe cleaner for a tail. Attach it to the pig.

7. Write 4 sentences in your math journal describing the geometry in your pig.

 Copymaster • *Common Core Math in Action* • © 2013 • Crystal Springs Books

Gobble! Gobble! Follow these directions to make a turkey.

1. Choose tan, gray, or brown paper for the head and body. Choose other colors for the other body parts.

2. Cut 4 similar circles for the head, body, and eyes.

3. Cut 2 congruent rectangles for legs.

4. Cut 4 congruent triangles for feathers.

5. Cut 2 congruent triangles for feet.

6. Cut 1 triangle for the comb.

7. Cut 1 rhombus for a beak.

8. Glue all the pieces together to create one handsome turkey. When you get to the beak, fold the rhombus so it looks like a triangle. Then glue half down and leave half sticking up.

9. In your math journal, write 4 sentences describing the geometry in your turkey.

Geome-Kitty *Use with Geometry Art, page 148.*

Meow! Meow! Make a purr-fectly wonderful kitty by following these directions.

1. Cut a circle for kitty's head.

2. Cut a larger circle for kitty's body.

3. Cut 2 congruent triangles for kitty's ears.

4. Cut 2 small congruent circles for kitty's eyes.

5. Cut 1 triangle for kitty's nose.

6. Cut 1 half-circle for kitty's mouth.

7. Cut 4 congruent rectangles for kitty's legs.

8. Cut 4 congruent circles for kitty's paws.

9. Glue the pieces together to assemble your kitty.

10. Write 3 sentences in your math journal about the geometry in your kitty.

 Copymaster • *Common Core Math in Action* • © 2013 • Crystal Springs Books

Pose this problem to your students and see how they solve it. You may read the problem to the children or distribute copies as an independent task. If you use this as an independent task, first be sure that your students can read the directions and understand the task. Provide 2 paper plates and a marker or scissors, and then read the problem. Give children time between the parts of the puzzle.

- -

Pizza Puzzle

Mom ordered two medium pizzas for the family. She cut one pizza into 2 equal pieces. She cut the other pizza into 4 equal pieces. Show Mom's cuts. You may cut the plates or draw lines on them.

Draw the pizza pieces here.

Mom gave Bill 2 pieces. She gave Pat 1 piece. Both children think the shares are fair.

Which pieces does Bill have?

Which piece does Pat have?

Can you show 2 pieces that are not fair shares?

____ I did this with my class.   ____ I did this with a group.   ____ I did this on my own.

How to Create a Splendid Giraffe *Use with Giraffe, page 152.*

Use brown, yellow, or tan paper for the giraffe's skin.

Use yellow, brown, or orange paper for the spots.

Use a ruler to measure and draw lines, scissors to cut, and glue or tape to attach the shapes.

1. Cut a rectangle that is 1 inch wide and 6 inches long for the neck.

2. Cut a 2-inch square for the head.

3. Cut a rectangle that is 3 inches wide and 6 inches long for the body.

4. Cut 4 thin congruent rectangles that are 6 inches long for legs.

5. Cut 2 congruent triangles or squares for ears.

6. Cut several hexagons of different sizes for spots.

7. Glue all the pieces to paper to make one splendid giraffe.

8. Give your giraffe a happy face.

Find out how your students are thinking about the shapes of equal shares of identical wholes. Provide some 1-inch tiles and either read the problem below, or make copies for independent work. If you do this as an independent task, first make sure that your students can read the problem independently.

- -

Tile Trouble

John has 13 square tiles. He says he can make 3 different rectangles with these 13 tiles. He will use all 13 tiles in each rectangle.

Vivian disagrees. She thinks John can make only 1 rectangle. He could turn that rectangle different ways, but it would still just be 1 long, skinny rectangle.

Who do you think is correct and why?

Vivian also tells John that if he uses only 12 of his squares, he could make many different rectangular shapes.

How many different rectangles can you make with 12 square tiles?

___ I did this with my class.   ___ I did this with a group.   ___ I did this on my own.

References & Resources

Children's Literature with Math Connections for Grades K–2

The following children's books, appropriate for grades K–2, are referenced within activities in this book.

Counting and Cardinality

Fish Eyes: A Book You Can Count On by Lois Ehlert

Operations and Algebraic Thinking

Quack and Count by Keith Baker
Ten Flashing Fireflies by Philemon Sturges
Ten Little Fish by Audrey Wood
Spunky Monkeys on Parade by Stuart J. Murphy
Ten Little Hermit Crabs by Lee Fox
Equal Shmequal by Virginia L. Kroll
A Pocket for Corduroy by Don Freeman
My Little Sister Ate One Hare by Bill Grossman
P. Bear's New Year's Party: A Counting Book by Paul Owen Lewis
One Duck Stuck by Phyllis Root
Panda Math by Ann Whitehead Nagda
Chrysanthemum by Kevin Henkes
Six-Dinner Sid by Inga Moore

Number and Operations in Base Ten

One Is a Snail, Ten Is a Crab: A Counting by Feet Book by April Pulley Sayre and Jeff Sayre
Centipede's 100 Shoes by Tony Ross
How Much Is a Million? by David M. Schwartz

Measurement and Data

The Best Bug Parade by Stuart J. Murphy
Caps for Sale by Esphyr Slobodkina
Hats Hats Hats by Ann Morris
The Grouchy Ladybug by Eric Carle
Inch by Inch by Leo Lionni
The Very Hungry Caterpillar by Eric Carle
Inchworm and a Half by Elinor J. Pinczes
How Big Is a Foot? by Rolf Myller

Actual Size by Steve Jenkins

Get Up and Go! by Stuart J. Murphy

Clocks and More Clocks by Pat Hutchins

Chimp Math: Learning About Time from a Baby Chimpanzee by Ann Whitehead Nagda and Cindy Bickel

Alexander, Who Used to Be Rich Last Sunday by Judith Viorst

Lemonade for Sale by Stuart J. Murphy

Tiger Math: Learning to Graph from a Baby Tiger by Ann Whitehead Nagda and Cindy Bickel

Geometry

Captain Invincible and the Space Shapes by Stuart J. Murphy

Town Mouse and Country Mouse, any version

Bigger, Better, Best! by Stuart J. Murphy

Ed Emberley's Picture Pie: A Cut and Paste Drawing Book by Ed Emberley

Coyote Steals the Blanket: A Ute Tale by Janet Stevens

Professional Books

Brooks, Jacqueline Grennon, and Martin G. Brooks. 1999. *In Search of Understanding: The Case for Constructivist Classrooms.* Rev ed. Alexandria, VA: ASCD.

Chambers, Donald L., ed. 2002. *Putting Research into Practice in the Elementary Grades: Readings from Journals of the NCTM.* Reston, VA: National Council of Teachers of Mathematics.

Copley, Juanita V., ed. 2000. *Mathematics in the Early Years.* Reston, VA: National Council of Teachers of Mathematics; Washington, DC: National Association for the Education of Young Children.

Ginsburg, Herbert P., and Sylvia Opper. 1988. *Piaget's Theory of Intellectual Development.* 3rd ed. Upper Saddle River, NJ: Pearson Higher Education.

Hiebert, James, et al. 2000. *Making Sense: Teaching and Learning Mathematics with Understanding.* Portsmouth, NH: Heinemann.

Kilpatrick, Jeremy, Jane Swafford, and Bradford Findell, eds. 2001. *Adding It Up: Helping Children Learn Mathematics.* Washington, DC: National Academies Press.

Marzano, Robert J. 2004. *Building Background Knowledge for Academic Achievement: Research on What Works in Schools.* Alexandria, VA: ASCD.

National Governors Association Center for Best Practices, Council of Chief State School Officers. 2010. *Common Core State Standards for Mathematics.* Washington, DC: National Governors Association Center for Best Practices, Council of Chief State School Officers.

Small, Marian. 2012. *Good Questions: Great Ways to Differentiate Mathematics Instruction.* 2nd ed. New York: Teachers College Press.

Van de Walle, John A., Karen S. Karp, and Jennifer M. Bay-Williams. 2003. *Elementary and Middle School Mathematics: Teaching Developmentally.* 8th ed. Upper Saddle River, NJ: Pearson.

Wadsworth, Barry J. 2003. *Piaget's Theory of Cognitive and Affective Development.* 5th ed. Upper Saddle River, NJ: Pearson.

Whitin, Phyllis, and David J. Whitin. 2000. *Math Is Language Too: Talking and Writing in the Mathematics Classroom.* Urbana, IL: National Council of Teachers of English.

Yee, Lee Peng, and Lee Ngan Hoe. 2009. *Teaching Primary School Mathematics: A Resource Book.* 2nd ed. Singapore: McGraw Hill Education (Asia).

Websites

Catherine Kuhns
www.catherinekuhns.com

Common Core State Standards Initiative
www.corestandards.org

Illustrative Mathematics
www.illustrativemathematics.org

K–5 Math Teaching Resources
www.k-5mathteachingresources.com

The Mathematics Common Core Toolbox
www.ccsstoolbox.com

MC^2, Marrie Lasater & Cindy Cliche
www.mathmc2.com

National Library of Virtual Manipulatives
nlvm.usu.edu

NCTM Illuminations
illuminations.nctm.org

Shodor
www.shodor.org

Index